THE ULTIMATE
PITTSBURGH STEELERS
TRIVIA BOOK

A Collection of Amazing Trivia Quizzes
and Fun Facts for Die-Hard Steelers Fans!

Ray Walker

Exclusive Free Book

Crazy Sports Stories

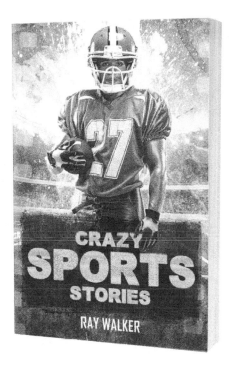

As a thank you for getting a copy of this book I would like to offer you a free copy of my book Crazy Sports Stories which comes packed with interesting stories from your favorite sports such as Football, Hockey, Baseball, Basketball and more.

Grab your free copy over at RayWalkerMedia.com/Bonus

CONTENTS

Introduction 1

Chapter 1: Origins & History 3

    Quiz Time! 3

    Quiz Answers 8

    Did You Know? 9

Chapter 2: Jerseys & Numbers 12

    Quiz Time! 12

    Quiz Answers 17

    Did You Know? 18

Chapter 3: Steelers Quarterbacks 20

    Quiz Time! 20

    Quiz Answers 26

    Did You Know? 27

Chapter 4: The Pass Catchers 29

    Quiz Time! 29

    Quiz Answers 35

Did You Know? 36

Chapter 5: Running Wild.. 38

Quiz Time! 38

Quiz Answers 44

Did You Know? 45

Chapter 6: In the Trenches.. 47

Quiz Time! 47

Quiz Answers 53

Did You Know? 54

Chapter 7: The Back Seven 57

Quiz Time! 57

Quiz Answers 63

Did You Know? 64

Chapter 8: Odds & Ends & Awards............................ 67

Quiz Time! 67

Quiz Answers 73

Did You Know? 74

Chapter 9: Nicknames 77

Quiz Time! 77

Quiz Answers 83

Did You Know? 84

Chapter 10: Alma Maters **88**

   Quiz Time! 88

   Quiz Answers 94

   Did You Know? 95

Chapter 11: In the Draft Room **99**

   Quiz Time! 99

   Quiz Answers 104

   Did You Know? 105

Chapter 12: The Trading Post **109**

   Quiz Time! 109

   Quiz Answers 115

   Did You Know? 116

Chapter 13: Super Bowl Special **120**

   Quiz Time! 120

   Quiz Answers 125

   Did You Know? 126

Conclusion **129**

INTRODUCTION

Every team boasts a group of passionate fans. These avid supporters develop a special bond with a team and they join forces to form a community of loyal, dedicated fanatics committed to rooting for their favorite players and coaches.

The Pittsburgh Steelers are one of the most decorated franchises in NFL history. Their rags-to-riches legacy, which includes six Super Bowl triumphs and an amazing home sellout streak that spanned over 40 years, has cemented a unique union between a storied franchise and its blue-collar fan base.

The mission of this book is to celebrate the men who transformed the Steelers into an NFL dynasty. From Art Rooney to Chuck Noll to legendary players like Mean Joe Greene, Terry Bradshaw, Franco Harris and Mel Blount – the collection of Hall of Fame talent that showcased their skills in Pittsburgh in the 1970s was truly unprecedented.

This fact-filled trivia book features an array of quizzes that will test your knowledge of Steelers history. Each chapter consists of multiple-choice and true-or-false questions, and a "Did You Know?" section with interesting team information.

1

How much do you really know about the Steelers? Whether you and your buddies decide to battle wits for bragging rights or make a friendly wager to see who the most knowledgeable fan really is, this incredible book will provide hours of entertainment to Steeler fanatics of all ages.

There are high expectations in Pittsburgh in 2020 with the return of quarterback Ben Roethlisberger. The team, which has one of the league's top defensive units, will be eyeing a return to the postseason. So, the next time you're watching the Steelers on television, use the information in this book to impress your family and friends with how much you know about the Steel Curtain and other great Pittsburgh squads.

CHAPTER 1:

ORIGINS & HISTORY

QUIZ TIME!

1. In which year was the Pittsburgh Steelers football team founded?

    a. 1930

    b. 1933

    c. 1939

    d. 1940

2. The Pittsburgh franchise was known as the Pirates during its first seven seasons.

    a. True

    b. False

3. Which player blocked a punt through the end zone for a safety that resulted in the franchise's first-ever points?

    a. Red Grange

    b. Bill Tanguay

    c. John "Cap" Oehler

    d. Angelo "Angie" Brovelli

4. During the inaugural NFL Draft in 1936, which player became Pittsburgh's first draft choice?

   a. William Shakespeare
   b. Larry Lutz
   c. Bob "Choo Choo" Train
   d. Bobby Grayson

5. Heinz Field is the current home of the Steelers. Where did Pittsburgh play its home games during its inaugural season?

   a. Shibe Park
   b. Forbes Field
   c. Polo Grounds
   d. Comiskey Park

6. The Steelers made All-American Byron "Whizzer" White the NFL's highest-paid player in 1938. How much was his contract?

   a. $13,000
   b. $17,500
   c. $10,000
   d. $15,800

7. The Steelers defeated the Philadelphia Eagles, 21-0, in their first postseason game ever in 1947.

   a. True
   b. False

8. Which legendary coach turned down the Steelers in 1969 before Chuck Noll was hired?

a. Joe Paterno

b. Tom Landry

c. Paul Brown

d. Weeb Ewbank

9. What was the name of the cheerleading team that rooted for the Steelers from 1961-1970?

a. Steel Queens

b. The Bumble Bees

c. Pitt Cheerleaders

d. Steelerettes

10. Which player scored the very first touchdown in Pittsburgh Steelers history?

a. Bill Dudley

b. Jerome Bettis

c. Martin Kottler

d. John Henry Johnson

11. Due to the war, the Steelers and Philadelphia Eagles merged rosters in 1943 to become the Steagles.

a. True

b. False

12. Which journalist was known as the "voice of the Pittsburgh Steelers" and helped invent the Terrible Towel?

a. Bob Prince

b. Myron Cope

c. Mike Lange

d. Bill Hillgrove

13. Pittsburgh drafted and cut which future Hall of Fame quarterback in 1955?

    a. Fran Tarkenton
    b. Bobby Layne
    c. Johnny Unitas
    d. Jim Hart

14. The Steelers "asteroid" logo that debuted in 1962 was based on the American Iron and Steel Institute's Steelmark.

    a. True
    b. False

15. Which Steeler legend became a long-time defensive coordinator for the Dallas Cowboys?

    a. Rocky Bleier
    b. Jack Ham
    c. Cal Hubbard
    d. Ernie Stautner

16. Who is the all-time leading scorer in franchise history?

    a. Franco Harris
    b. Gary Anderson
    c. Antonio Brown
    d. John Henry Johnson

17. How many Steelers are enshrined in the Pro Football Hall of Fame?

    a. 18
    b. 20
    c. 15
    d. 24

18. Since 1966, Pittsburgh has held its training camp at which location?

    a. Chatham University
    b. St. Vincent College
    c. Gettysburg College
    d. Franklin & Marshall College

19. Pittsburgh is the only NFL team to win back-to-back Super Bowl titles twice.

    a. True
    b. False

20. What is the name of the Steelers' official mascot?

    a. Iron Rebel
    b. Silver Fox
    c. Steely McBeam
    d. Buzz Steel

QUIZ ANSWERS

1. B - 1933

2. A - True

3. C - John "Cap" Oehler

4. A - William Shakespeare

5. B - Forbes Field

6. D - $15,800

7. B - False

8. A - Joe Paterno

9. D - Steelerettes

10. C - Martin Kottler

11. A - True

12. B - Myron Cope

13. C - Johnny Unitas

14. A - True

15. D - Ernie Stautner

16. B - Gary Anderson

17. D - 24

18. B – St. Vincent College

19. A - True

20. C - Steely McBeam

DID YOU KNOW?

1. Steelers founder Art Rooney was also a standout athlete who was recruited to play both college football and professional baseball. The Pittsburgh native, who was invited to join the 1920 U.S. Olympic boxing team, founded his own semi-professional football team at the age of 19.

2. The Pittsburgh franchise has had several names since its inception in 1933. The team was called the Pirates until 1940, when the organization was rebranded the Steelers. During World War II, the team merged with the Philadelphia Eagles in 1943 and was known as the Steagles. The following year, the Steelers merged with the Chicago Cardinals to form Card-Pitt, the only winless squad in team history.

3. The Steelers were one of a handful of franchises that provide African-American players with trendsetting opportunities. Besides hiring Lowell Perry as the NFL's first African-American assistant coach in 1957, the Steelers' Joe Gilliam was the first African-American quarterback to start an NFL season opener in 1973.

4. The Steelers' 1974 draft haul of four future Hall-of-Famers is considered the best draft in NFL history. Pittsburgh drafted Lynn Swann, Jack Lambert, John Stallworth and Mike Webster to put the finishing touches on one of the league's greatest dynasties.

5. The Pittsburgh Steelers and the Dallas Cowboys are the only two franchises with three consecutive head coaches who won Super Bowl titles. Chuck Noll, Bill Cowher and Mike Tomlin all captured Vince Lombardi trophies to match the Cowboys' trio of Tom Landry, Jimmy Johnson and Barry Switzer.

6. The first scheduled regular-season NFL game at Heinz Field was postponed due to the September 11 attacks. The Steelers opened the new facility on October 7 with a 16-7 victory over the Cincinnati Bengals. Quarterback Kordell Stewart scampered eight yards for the first touchdown in the stadium.

7. The Steelers, who are celebrating their 88th season in 2020, are the oldest franchise in the American Football Conference (AFC). Although Pittsburgh struggled mightily during its early years, the team has won eight AFC championships and six Super Bowl crowns since 1970.

8. Because athletic contests on Sundays were prohibited by strict blue laws in Pennsylvania, the franchise played its first four home games in 1933 on Wednesday nights. Also, to avoid competing with more popular sporting events, the Pirates played numerous home games at neutral sites away from Forbes Field.

9. The Steelers Hall of Honor was established in 2017 to recognize the franchise's outstanding players, coaches and contributors. The Hall of Honor had 36 members heading into the 2020 season, including 2019 inductees TE/T Larry

Brown (1971-1984), coach Bill Cowher (1992-2006), TE Elbie Nickel (1947-1957) and WR Hines Ward (1998-2011).

10. Chuck Noll won two NFL Championships as a player with the Cleveland Browns before becoming the architect of a Steelers dynasty that won four Super Bowl titles in six seasons. He became the first NFL coach to win four Vince Lombardi Trophies and he spent 23 years at the helm of the Steelers football team.

CHAPTER 2:

JERSEYS & NUMBERS

QUIZ TIME!

1. The Steelers retired number 70 in 1964 to honor franchise icon Ernie Stautner. Who is the only other player to wear number 70 before it was retired?

   a. Gil Duggan
   b. Al Wistert
   c. Mike Haggerty
   d. Paul Younger

2. Which player had the longest tenure wearing the same jersey?

   a. #1 - Gary Anderson
   b. #47 - Mel Blount
   c. #52 - Mike Webster
   d. #70 - Ernie Stautner

3. Five players who wore number 35 for the Pirates/Steelers have been elected to the Hall of Fame.

   a. True
   b. False

4. What was the nickname given to the Steelers' new uniform jersey that debuted in 1966?

    a. Clowns
    b. Gold Stars
    c. Batman
    d. Golden Triangle

5. A pair of star wide receivers each wore number 25 for Pittsburgh. Who were these two receivers?

    a. Ray Mathews & Ronnie Shanklin
    b. Jim Smith & Frank Lewis
    c. Louis Lipps & Dave Smith
    d. Jeff Graham & Barry Pearson

6. Besides the Steelers, which other NFL team has player's uniform numbers on both the front and back of their helmets?

    a. Washington Redskins
    b. Chicago Bears
    c. New York Giants
    d. Kansas City Chiefs

7. Before Tommy Maddux wearing number 8 in 2001, when was the last time the number was issued?

    a. 1937
    b. 1939
    c. 1940
    d. 1944

8. Joe Womack rushed for more yards than any other Steelers player who wore number 32.

a. True

b. False

9. 21 players have worn number 82 for the Steelers. Which of them caught the most passes?

   a. Yancey Thigpen

   b. Bobby Shaw

   c. John Hilton

   d. John Stallworth

10. Which of the following Steeler players wore number 00 on his jersey?

    a. Dick Riffle

    b. Kent Graham

    c. Johnny Clement

    d. Dick Leftridge

11. Before wearing number 84, Steelers receiver Antonio Brown wore number 14 during the preseason of his rookie year

    a. True

    b. False

12. The most popular numbers in Steelers history have been worn by a total of 30 players. Which numbers saw this most widespread use?

    a. 10 & 12

    b. 85 & 88

    c. 56 & 58

    d. 72 & 75

13. Only four Steeler players aside from QB Bubby Brister have worn number 6 for the franchise. Who are these players?

    a. Thomas Cosgrove, Chester Johnson, Jim Elliott, Shaun Suisham

    b. Warren Heller, George Kiick, Andy Tomasic, Jon Kolb

    c. Maurice Bray, Les Dodson, Jim Levey, Greg Anderson

    d. Mel Pittman, Dave Trout, Warren Heller, Bobby Walden

14. Since the 1930s, no Steeler has ever been courageous enough to wear unlucky number 13 on the back of his jersey.

    a. True

    b. False

15. Franchise icon Mean Joe Greene wore number 75 for much of his Steelers career. What other number did he briefly wear during his rookie season?

    a. 70

    b. 72

    c. 77

    d. 78

16. Although the Steelers have several jerseys that are "unofficially" retired, which two jersey numbers are "officially" retired?

    a. 58 & 75

    b. 12 & 47

    c. 70 & 75

    d. 47 & 70

17. The Steelers had several logos in the early part of their history. Which of the following logos were never used by the franchise?

    a. Crest of Pittsburgh
    b. Construction worker punting a football on a steel beam
    c. Steel worker spiking a football
    d. A football with Pittsburgh's smoggy skyline

18. Terry Bradshaw has thrown 212 of the 218 touchdown passes thrown by four Steelers quarterbacks who wore number 12.

    a. True
    b. False

19. Defensive end George Tarasovic was issued more jersey numbers than any player in team history. How many different numbers did he wear?

    a. 3
    b. 5
    c. 7
    d. 8

20. What former Steelers defensive back wore number 21 before becoming a successful NFL head coach?

    a. Jim Shorter
    b. Greg Lee
    c. Deon Figures
    d. Tony Dungy

QUIZ ANSWERS

1. B - Al Wistert

2. C - Mike Webster

3. A - True

4. C - Batman

5. A - Ray Mathews & Ronnie Shanklin

6. C - New York Giants

7. C - 1940

8. B - False

9. D - John Stallworth

10. C - Johnny Clement

11. B - False

12. B - 85 & 88

13. A - T. Cosgrove, C. Johnson, J. Elliott, S. Suisham

14. B - False

15. B - 72

16. C - 70 & 75

17. C - Steel worker spiking football

18. A - True

19. B - 5

20. D - Tony Dungy

DID YOU KNOW?

1. The Steelers retired Ernie Stautner's number 70 jersey in 1964, and then went 50 years before retiring Mean Joe Green's number 75 jersey in 2014.

2. Pittsburgh has worn black and gold uniforms since the club's inception in 1933. However, due to a player shortage because of World War II, the Steelers used the colors green and white in 1943, when they merged with the Philadelphia Eagles to form the "Steagles."

3. The team wore a helmet decal with "DD" during the 2019 season to pay tribute to former wide receivers coach Darryl Drake, who passed away suddenly during training camp.

4. The first player to wear a number in the 70s for the Steelers was end Tom Brown, who wore number 76 in 1942. He attended the College of William & Mary and caught 4 passes for 69 yards in nine NFL games.

5. During the NFL's 75th anniversary celebration in 1994, the Steelers wore jerseys that featured the crest of the City of Pittsburgh on the front. These replicas were originally worn in a few games during the team's inaugural season in 1933.

6. Marion Motley wore two numbers, 36 and 37, while wrapping up his career with the Steelers in 1955. He became the second black player voted into the Pro Football Hall of Fame in 1968.

7. Pittsburgh center Ray Mansfield, who wore numbers 56 and 73 during his 13-year career with the Steelers, played in an amazing 182 consecutive games. In his final season in 1976, he kicked an extra point in a playoff game after the regular kicker was injured.

8. The first player ever drafted by the franchise, William "Bill" Shakespeare, was never issued a jersey in 1936 because he opted for a career in business. He was a consensus first-team All-American halfback at Notre Dame in 1935.

9. Bobby Layne and John Henry Johnson both took their favorite jersey numbers from other players. Layne took number 22 from Richie McCabe, while Johnson took number 35 from Rudy Hayes.

10. Linebacker Joe Williams became the first player to wear number 97 for the Steelers in 1987. He played collegiate football at Grambling State and played in the Arena Football League.

CHAPTER 3:

STEELERS QUARTERBACKS

QUIZ TIME!

1. Who was the first Pittsburgh-area native player to start at quarterback for the Steelers since Terry Hanratty started a few games in 1969?

    a. Charlie Batch
    b. Mike Kruczek
    c. Jim Miller
    d. Reggie Collier

2. Bobby Layne had only one winning record during his five seasons under center for the Steelers.

    a. True
    b. False

3. Three Pittsburgh Steelers quarterbacks have thrown for at least 5 touchdowns in a game. Which quarterback did not achieve this rare feat?

    a. Ben Roethlisberger
    b. Mark Malone

c. Bobby Layne

d. Terry Bradshaw

4. Which dual-threat quarterback earned the nickname "Slash" as a rookie because of his receiving skills?

a. Joe Gilliam

b. Kordell Stewart

c. Leon Pense

d. Anthony Wright

5. Cliff Stoudt set an NFL record for the most games to start a career on the active roster without appearing in an official game. How many games did he watch from the sidelines before making his league debut?

a. 39

b. 47

c. 56

d. 61

6. Terry Bradshaw won 14 of 19 postseason games and had a 4-0 record in the Super Bowl.

a. True

b. False

7. What team signed Pittsburgh quarterback Neil O'Donnell to a $25 million free-agent contract just one month after the Steelers lost in Super Bowl XXX?

a. Arizona Cardinals

b. New York Jets

c. Tennessee Titans

d. Cincinnati Bengals

8. Which Steelers quarterback threw 46 interceptions in his first 27 games after being the first overall draft choice?

    a. Len Dawson
    b. Terry Bradshaw
    c. Ted Marchibroda
    d. Byron "Whizzer" White

9. Who was the first quarterback in Steelers history to complete over 80% of his passes (minimum 20 attempts) in a single game?

    a. Earl Morrall
    b. Allie Sherman
    c. Mark Malone
    d. Todd Blackledge

10. Ben Roethlisberger was the first quarterback in NFL history to have beaten 31 different NFL teams.

    a. True
    b. False

11. How old was Tommy Maddox when he became the youngest NFL player to complete a touchdown pass since 1950.

    a. 19
    b. 20
    c. 21
    d. 22

12. Which former Steeler is one of just two quarterbacks in NFL history (Ken Stabler) to have a career winning percentage

above .600 while also throwing at least 10 more interceptions than touchdowns.

a. Steve Bono

b. Byron Leftwich

c. David Woodley

d. Scott Campbell

13. Which Steelers player was involved in a brawl against the Cleveland Browns that resulted in him being hit in the head with a helmet?

a. Landry Jones

b. Devlin Hodges

c. Joshua Dobbs

d. Mason Rudolph

14. Tommy Maddox became a used car salesman before joining the Arena Football League en route to winning the NFL's 2002 Comeback Player of the Year award.

a. True

b. False

15. Which Pittsburgh quarterback posted a 13-0 record as a starter during his rookie season?

a. Jim Finks

b. Terry Bradshaw

c. Bobby Layne

d. Ben Roethlisberger

16. In 1968, the Steelers traded quarterback Bill Nelsen and defensive back Jim Bradshaw to the Browns for defensive

tackle Frank Parker, an undisclosed draft choice and a quarterback. Who was the quarterback that Pittsburgh acquired?

    a. Dick Shiner

    b. Kent Nix

    c. Rudy Bukich

    d. Terry Hanratty

17. Which former Steelers quarterback later became the offensive coordinator for the Pittsburgh Power of the Arena Football League?

    a. Bubby Brister

    b. Dennis Dixon

    c. Mike Tomczak

    d. Jim Miller

18. Besides being credited with creating the two-minute drill, Bobby Layne retired as one of the last players to wear a helmet without a facemask.

    a. True

    b. False

19. Which player has the third-longest tenure in team history for a quarterback, behind only Terry Bradshaw and Ben Roethlisberger?

    a. Landry Jones

    b. Charlie Batch

    c. Kordell Stewart

    d. Neil O'Donnell

20. Mark Malone, a quarterback, held the team record for the longest touchdown reception for several years before it was broken. How long was his touchdown catch?

    a. 88 yards

    b. 89 yards

    c. 90 yards

    d. 95 yards

QUIZ ANSWERS

1. A - Charlie Batch

2. B - False

3. C - Bobby Layne

4. B - Kordell Stewart

5. C - 56

6. A - True

7. B - New York Jets

8. B - Terry Bradshaw

9. C - Mark Malone

10. B - False

11. C - 21

12. C - David Woodley

13. D - Mason Rudolph

14. B - False

15. D - Ben Roethlisberger

16. A - Dick Shiner

17. C - Mike Tomczak

18. A - True

19. B - Charlie Batch

20. C - 90 yards

DID YOU KNOW?

1. University of Alabama standout Tony Holm became the first starting quarterback of the Pirates/Steelers franchise in 1933. The All-American played four seasons in the NFL and was also a punter.

2. The Steelers drafted tailback Bill Dudley with the first overall pick in the 1942 draft. He is the only player in the history of the league with a rushing touchdown, touchdown reception, punt return for touchdown, kickoff return for touchdown, interception return for touchdown, fumble return for a touchdown and a touchdown pass.

3. Although Bruce Gradkowski spent three seasons with the Steelers, the Pittsburgh native and former Toledo quarterback only saw action briefly in one regular season game.

4. Terry Bradshaw lost his starting job temporarily to Joe Gilliam in 1974 but rebounded to lead the Steelers to their first Super Bowl title. He tossed a touchdown pass to Lynn Swann to beat the Oakland Raiders in the AFC Championship Game and threw another late scoring pass against the Minnesota Vikings to capture the Vince Lombardi Trophy.

5. Ben Roethlisberger became the youngest quarterback to win the Super Bowl in 2006 at the age of 23 despite a horrible performance that included the lowest passing rating in Super Bowl history by a winning quarterback.

6. Only three NFL quarterbacks – Cam Newton (58), Steve Young (43) and Jack Kemp (40) – have rushed for more touchdowns than former Steeler Kordell Stewart, who tallied 38 scores on the ground during his 11-year career.

7. Backup quarterback Byron Leftwich had two stints with the Steelers. The seventh overall pick in the 2003 NFL Draft signed a one-year deal with Pittsburgh in 2008 and, after suiting up for the Tampa Bay Buccaneers in 2009, he was traded back to Pittsburgh the next year. However, he missed the entire 2011 season with a broken arm before ending his career as a Steeler the following year.

8. Former Steelers quarterback Bubby Brister, who won two Super Bowl rings with the Denver Broncos, played one season of minor league baseball for the Bristol Tigers after being drafted in the fourth round by the Detroit Tigers. He started 57 games for Pittsburgh, throwing for 51 touchdowns and 10,104 yards.

9. Neil O'Donnell quietly led the Steelers to the playoffs in all four seasons that he was the starting quarterback. He posted a 37-16 record from 1992-95 with 57 touchdown passes and led Pittsburgh to Super Bowl XXX during his final year with the franchise.

10. Washington Redskins' 1964 seventh-round draft pick Dick Shiner was traded to Pittsburgh in 1968 and went on to become the Steelers starting quarterback for parts of two seasons. He guided the team to a win over the Detroit Lions in the 1969 season-opening game to help Chuck Noll collect his first NFL victory.

CHAPTER 4:

THE PASS CATCHERS

QUIZ TIME!

1. Which legendary Steelers receiver was born in South Korea to an American father and a Korean mother?

    a. Amara Darboh
    b. Ron Shanklin
    c. Hines Ward
    d. Saeed Blacknall

2. Hines Ward's stock dipped in the 1998 NFL Draft because it was discovered that he did not have an anterior cruciate ligament (ACL) in one of his legs.

    a. True
    b. False

3. The Steelers' 1974 NFL Draft is considered one of the best in league history and included four eventual Hall-of-Famers. Which of the following receivers were drafted along with Mike Webster, John Stallworth and Jack Lambert?

a. Jim Smith

b. Lynn Swann

c. Louis Lipps

d. Ray Mathews

4. John Stallworth earned NFL Comeback Player of the Year honors in 1984 after a stellar season in which he compiled a career-high 1,395 receiving yards. How many receptions did he have that year?

a. 70

b. 75

c. 80

d. 85

5. Santonio Holmes was named Super Bowl XLIII MVP, becoming the third Pittsburgh receiver to win the award. Which two receivers were also named MVP of the Super Bowl?

a. Lynn Swann & Hines Ward

b. Hines Ward & Antonio Brown

c. Antonio Brown & Emmanuel Sanders

d. Lynn Swann & John Stallworth

6. Lynn Swann credited his success on the football field to his background in dance. A graceful receiver with soft hands, Swann was featured in a Pittsburgh dance studio during a 1981 interview on Mr. Rogers' Neighborhood.

a. True

b. False

7. In a 2015 game against the Oakland Raiders, Antonio Brown set an NFL record for most receiving yards without having a touchdown reception. How many yards did Brown post that historic day?

    a. 200
    b. 233
    c. 257
    d. 284

8. Which rookie receiver broke the NFL record for punt return yardage by a rookie, hauled in 45 passes for 9 touchdowns and was named the 1984 Offensive Rookie of the Year?

    a. Yancey Thigpen
    b. Louis Lipps
    c. Santonio Holmes
    d. Antwaan Randle El

9. Besides being the youngest player selected in the 2017 Draft, JuJu Smith-Schuster also set an NFL record during his rookie season for the number of touchdowns before his 21st birthday. How many touchdowns did he have?

    a. 3
    b. 4
    c. 5
    d. 6

10. Who is the only wide receiver in Super Bowl history to throw a touchdown pass?

a. Mike Wallace

b. Hines Ward

c. Antwaan Randle El

d. Emmanuel Sanders

11. Hall of Fame receiver John Stallworth is the only former Steelers player who is also a part-owner of the franchise.

a. True

b. False

12. Pittsburgh drafted a pair of productive wide receivers in the third and sixth rounds of the 2010 NFL Draft. Which two talented receivers were drafted by the Steelers?

a. Arnaz Battle & Yancey Thigpen

b. Emmanuel Sanders & Antonio Brown

c. Martavis Bryant & Louis Lipps

d. Jerricho Cotchery & Charles Johnson

13. Hines Ward combined with another wide receiver to give the Steelers their first pair of 1,000-yard receivers during both the 2001 and 2002 seasons. Who was the receiver that also tallied back-to-back 1000-yard seasons?

a. Frank Lewis

b. Mike Wallace

c. Santonio Holmes

d. Plaxico Burress

14. Mike Wallace tallied more 100-yard games than any other receiver in 2010. How many games did he post with more than 100 receiving yards?

a. 5

b. 6

c. 7

d. 8

15. During his second season in the league, Antonio Brown became the second player in NFL history to collect more than 1,000 yards receiving and returning in the same year.

    a. True

    b. False

16. The NFL suspended this speedy Steelers wide receiver for the entire 2016 NFL season for violating the league's substance abuse policy. Who was this receiver?

    a. Markus Wheaton

    b. Dwight Stone

    c. Martavis Bryant

    d. Plaxico Burress

17. In 1998, a former Steelers wide receiver inked the largest contract ever given to a receiver. He went on to play his final three seasons with the Houston Oilers and helped the team (now known as the Tennessee Titans) reach Super Bowl XXXIV.

    a. Eli Rogers

    b. Yancey Thigpen

    c. Charles Johnson

    d. Andre Hastings

18. Hines Ward is considered one of the greatest receivers in NFL history, but he did not have many seasons with 100

receptions. How many seasons did he haul in 100 or more passes?

    a. 0

    b. 1

    c. 2

    d. 3

19. JuJu Smith-Schuster competed in the Snoop Youth Football League and was coached by legendary rapper Snoop Dogg, who nicknamed him "SportsCenter" after the ESPN highlights show.

    a. True

    b. False

20. Which former Pittsburgh legend became the only receiver in NFL history to record five receptions and at least 50 yards in every game for a full season?

    a. Plaxico Burress

    b. Hines Ward

    c. John Stallworth

    d. Antonio Brown

QUIZ ANSWERS

1. C - Hines Ward

2. A - True

3. B - Lynn Swann

4. C - 80

5. A - Lynn Swann & Hines Ward

6. A - True

7. D - 284

8. B - Louis Lipps

9. C - 5

10. C - Antwaan Randle El

11. A - True

12. B - Emmanuel Sanders & Antonio Brown

13. D - Plaxico Burress

14. C - 7

15. B - False

16. C - Martavis Bryant

17. B - Yancey Thigpen

18. B - 1

19. A - True

20. D - Antonio Brown

DID YOU KNOW?

1. Although he was only a third-round pick, Hines Ward started an incredible 83 consecutive games for the Steelers and retired as the franchise leader in receptions (1,000), yards (12,083) and touchdowns (85).

2. Steelers Hall-of-Famer Lynn Swann was the Republican nominee for Governor of Pennsylvania in the 2006 election. He lost the race 60% to 40% to incumbent Governor Ed Rendell.

3. John Stallworth was one of the greatest postseason receivers in NFL history. He tallied 12 touchdown catches and put together a string of 17 consecutive playoff games with at least one reception. The Alabama native also found the end zone in eight straight postseason games, from 1978 through 1983.

4. Antonio Brown wore "The Hippo" costume and competed on the American version of The Masked Singer in 2019. He performed Bobby Brown's "My Prerogative" and was eliminated during the first episode of the show.

5. Besides being the first NFL player to have a pair of offensive touchdowns of at least 97 yards, JuJu Smith-Schuster is also the youngest player to reach 2,500 career receiving yards.

6. A star player at Grambling State, former Steelers first-round draft pick Frank Lewis scored 42 collegiate

touchdowns and was inducted into the Black College Football Hall of Fame in 2019.

7. Pittsburgh receiver Weegie Thompson got his nickname from his father, whose little brother could not pronounce his name, Willis. It came out Weegie and both he and his father used the nickname.

8. Cedrick Wilson won a Super Bowl ring in 2006 with the Steelers and achieved a rare feat by winning a championship ring at three different levels - high school, college and professional.

9. Former Pittsburgh receiver Eli Rogers was drafted by the DC Defenders in the 2020 XFL supplemental draft. In four NFL seasons, he caught 78 passes for 822 yards and four touchdowns.

10. Lynn Swann appeared as a panelist on the television game show, "To Tell the Truth," on NBC before becoming the host. However, he was replaced by Alex Trebek after 14 weeks.

CHAPTER 5:

RUNNING WILD

QUIZ TIME!

1. Who broke the franchise record for most receptions in a game by a running back with 13 catches against the Indianapolis Colts?

    a. James Conner

    b. Le'Veon Bell

    c. Jaylen Samuels

    d. DeAngelo Williams

2. Which Steelers running back was diagnosed with Hodgkin's lymphoma in 2015, but announced the following year on Twitter that he was cancer-free?

    a. Jonathan Dwyer

    b. Jaylen Samuels

    c. James Conner

    d. Rashard Mendenhall

3. Tom Tracy rushed for 2,717 yards and 15 touchdowns in 60 games with the Steelers and was named to the Pro Bowl on two occasions.

a. True

b. False

4. Steelers running back Rocky Bleier missed 10 games in 1979, which opened the door for another back to join Franco Harris in the backfield. Who was the running back that ran for 585 yards and 6 touchdowns that season?

   a. John "French" Fuqua

   b. Frank Pollard

   c. Earnest Jackson

   d. Sidney Thornton

5. Mercury Morris and Larry Csonka became the first backfield duo to both rush for 1,000 yards in the same season in 1972, during the Miami Dolphins' undefeated season. However, a pair of Pittsburgh running backs achieved the same feat four years later. Who were these talented Steelers running backs?

   a. Willie Asbury & Frank Pollard

   b. Barry Foster & Merril Hoge

   c. John Fuqua & Franco Harris

   d. Franco Harris & Rocky Bleier

6. Barry Foster had a career year in 1992 and set a franchise record for the most rushing yards in a single season. How many yards did he gain?

   a. 1,494

   b. 1,665

   c. 1,690

   d. 1,718

7. Franco Harris rushed for 1,000 yards in eight different seasons to break Jim Brown's record and was also chosen for nine consecutive Pro Bowls from 1972 to 1980.

   a. True
   b. False

8. Priest Holmes was the first undrafted running back to run for over 1,200 yards in a single season in NFL history. Which Pittsburgh ball carrier was the second player to accomplish this feat?

   a. Willie Parker
   b. Amos Zereoué
   c. Leroy Thompson
   d. Tim Worley

9. Which former Steelers running back was forced to retire due to brain injury in 1994 after suffering a concussion that caused him to stop breathing?

   a. Spencer Nigh
   b. Merril Hoge
   c. Ralph Webb
   d. Tim Worley

10. Which running back nicknamed "The Bus" and "The Closer" rushed for 10,571 yards and 78 touchdowns in his 10 seasons with the Steelers?

   a. Jerome Bettis
   b. Eric Pegram
   c. DeAngelo Williams
   d. Le'Veon Bell

11. Barry Foster came out of retirement in 1995 and signed a $1 million deal with the Cincinnati Bengals. However, two days later, the 26-year-old running back changed his mind and retired again.

    a. True
    b. False

12. Which football team did Bam Morris sign with in 2006 after he was released from prison for drug trafficking?

    a. Detroit Lions
    b. Katy Copperheads
    c. Chicago Bears
    d. Kansas City Chiefs

13. Which Pittsburgh Steelers running back announced his retirement on Facebook?

    a. Barry Foster
    b. John Fuqua
    c. DeAngelo Williams
    d. Walter Abercrombie

14. In 2018, the Pittsburgh Steelers signed free agent running back Trey Edmunds, which reunited him with his cousin Terrell Edmunds.

    a. True
    b. False

15. Walter Abercrombie was a standout running back at Baylor University who was selected 12th overall in the 1982 draft. How many touchdowns did he score during his six-year career with the Steelers?

a. 18

b. 22

c. 29

d. 33

16. West Virginia running back Amos Zereoué was selected in the third round by Pittsburgh in 1999. Zereoué was born in which country?

a. Nigeria

b. Ghana

c. South Africa

d. Ivory Coast

17. Who was the running back that Terry Bradshaw was targeting with a pass that led to the Immaculate Reception?

a. Rocky Bleier

b. John Fuqua

c. Dick Hoak

d. Jonathan Dwyer

18. Earnest Jackson attended Texas A&M and was named to his second Pro Bowl in 1986 after leading the Steelers in rushing. How many yards did Jackson gain?

a. 883

b. 910

c. 946

d. 982

19. In a 2015 contest, DeAngelo Williams was fined nearly $6,000 for wearing eye black that read "Find the Cure" in honor of breast cancer awareness.

a. True

b. False

20. Which 26-year-old former Pittsburgh running back abruptly retired from the NFL in 2014, saying, "Football was pretty cool, but I don't want to play anymore. I want to travel the world and write!"

a. Willie Parker

b. Rashard Mendenhall

c. Jonathan Dwyer

d. Willie Asbury

QUIZ ANSWERS

1. C - Jaylen Samuels

2. C - James Conner

3. A - True

4. D - Sidney Thornton

5. D - Franco Harris & Rocky Bleier

6. C - 1,690

7. A - True

8. A - Willie Parker

9. B - Merril Hoge

10. A - Jerome Bettis

11. A - True

12. B - Katy Copperheads

13. C - DeAngelo Williams

14. B - False

15. C - 29

16. D - Ivory Coast

17. B - John Fuqua

18. B - 910

19. A - True

20. B - Rashard Mendenhall

DID YOU KNOW?

1. Dick Hoak spent 10 seasons with the Steelers and formed a powerful ground attack with Hall-of-Famer John Henry Johnson. He led the team in rushing on three different occasions and served as the running backs coach for Pittsburgh for 35 seasons.

2. College teammates Franco Harris and Lydell Mitchell co-own the Super Bakery, which makes the popular Super Donut. The company produces nutrition-oriented foods for schoolchildren in the eastern United States.

3. A Hall of Fame fullback who led the Steelers in rushing from 1961-1964, John Henry Johnson played only six seasons for Pittsburgh but gained 4,381 rushing yards and scored 26 touchdowns. He also played for San Francisco and Detroit and finished his career with 6,803 yards and 48 touchdowns.

4. Frank Pollard played nine seasons for the Steelers but is known more for his track and field heroics during high school. The 19-year-old senior set a new Texas high school scoring record by capturing first place in the discus, shot put and the 100-yard and 220-yard sprints.

5. Although Preston Pearson was one of the first running backs to be known as a third-down receiving back, Leroy Thompson was also an adept receiver out of the backfield. He tallied 74 receptions in three seasons with the Steelers

and ended his six-year career with 153 catches for 1,193 yards and 5 touchdowns.

6. Before sitting out the 2018 season, Pittsburgh running back Le'Veon Bell enjoyed a dominant 2017 campaign. He posted a league-high 321 carries for 1,291 yards, while also tallying 655 yards on 85 receptions.

7. Steelers running back Rocky Bleier wrote a book, *Fighting Back: The Rocky Bleier Story*, which was made into a 1980 television movie starring Robert Ulrich, Richard Herd and Art Carney. The cast also included Mean Joe Greene and other players who portrayed themselves.

8. Pittsburgh Hall of Fame running back Franco Harris has numerous business endeavors, including part-ownership of the Pittsburgh Passion, a full-contact women's American football team that won back-to-back Independent Women's Football League (IWFL) championships in 2014 and 2015.

9. James Conner, who was the eighth running back chosen in the 2017 draft, had the best-selling NFL jersey in July of the same year, topping all rookies, as well as star quarterbacks Tom Brady and Dak Prescott.

10. Jonathan Dwyer failed a drug test at the 2010 NFL Scouting Combine after testing positive for amphetamines. But the test results were voided by the NFL after it was discovered that the positive test stemmed from the attention deficit disorder (ADD) medicine that he must take.

CHAPTER 6:

IN THE TRENCHES

QUIZ TIME!

1. Jon Kolb, like many of the Steeler players of the 1970s, had his own collection of fans. What were his fans called?

    a. Kolb's Klub

    b. Kolb's Kowboys

    c. Kolb's Korner

    d. Kolb's Army

2. Offensive tackle Tunch Ilkin was a two-time Pro Bowl selection who started 143 games for the Steelers. However, he is known as being the first person to play in the National Football League who was born in what country?

    a. Turkey

    b. Greece

    c. Israel

    d. Ukraine

3. Larry Brown played tight end and offensive tackle for the Steelers and was one of just 21 players to suit up in all the Steelers' first four Super Bowl titles.

a. True

b. False

4. What was the medical condition that almost derailed the football career of legendary Pittsburgh offensive guard Alan Faneca at the age of 15?

   a. Diabetes

   b. Epilepsy

   c. Lyme carditis

   d. Measles

5. Pittsburgh drafted David DeCastro in the first round of the 2012 NFL Draft. He was the first offensive guard taken in the first round by the Steelers in a decade. Who was the offensive guard that the Steelers drafted in 2002?

   a. Rich Tylski

   b. Brendan Stai

   c. Keydrick Vincent

   d. Kendall Simmons

6. An All-American offensive lineman out of Penn State, Jeff Hartings won three Super Bowl rings with the Steelers and New England Patriots.

   a. True

   b. False

7. What was the nickname of Steelers guard Gerry Mullins, who started on four Super Bowl-winning teams?

   a. Moon

   b. Doc

c. Fox

d. Professor

8. Pittsburgh center Maurkice Pouncey has an identical twin brother, Mike, who was drafted by the Miami Dolphins in the first round of the 2011 NFL Draft. What position does his brother play?

    a. Guard

    b. Linebacker

    c. Center

    d. Defensive tackle

9. Who was the center who developed into a seven-time Pro Bowl selection after replacing legendary Steelers center Mike Webster when Webster signed with the Kansas City Chiefs?

    a. Sean Mahan

    b. Dermontti Dawson

    c. Roger Duffy

    d. Jeff Hartings

10. Alejandro Villanueva became the first Steelers offensive lineman to catch a touchdown pass on a fake field goal in 2018.

    a. True

    b. False

11. Frank Varrichione helped Notre Dame share the 1953 national championship. He played 11 seasons in the NFL, was a five-time Pro Bowl selection and signed a hefty

contract with the Steelers in 1955. How much was his contract worth?

a. $3,500

b. $6,000

c. $8,000

d. $8,500

12. Former Steelers lineman Duval Love played 12 seasons in the NFL despite being a late-round draft choice. How many players were chosen before Love in the 1985 draft?

a. 157

b. 190

c. 228

d. 273

13. Which Pittsburgh 12th-round draft pick won six NCAA wrestling titles and went 3-2 as a mixed martial arts fighter?

a. Ramon Foster

b. Doug Legursky

c. Carlton Haselrig

d. Chris Kemoeatu

14. Craig Wolfley, a fifth-round draft pick by the Steelers in 1980, also competed in a variety of other sports. Which of the following activities below did Wolfley not participate in?

a. Boxing

b. Weightlifting

c. Sumo wrestling

d. Flag football

15. Pittsburgh legend Mike Webster lived out of his pickup truck for a short period after his playing career ended while suffering from amnesia, dementia, depression, and acute bone and muscular pain before his death.

    a. True
    b. False

16. Which Steeler lineman who admitted using steroids in college, was blackballed by the NFL for his outspoken views on performance-enhancing drugs?

    a. Terry Long
    b. Steve Courson
    c. Tyrone McGriff
    d. Jim Clack

17. A star player at Notre Dame, which offensive tackle played for the Steelers from 1955 to 1960 and averaged 9.2 yards as a part-time kick returner?

    a. Ray Pinney
    b. Ed Bernet
    c. Frank Varrichione
    d. Dick Tomlinson

18. How many games did Ray Pinney, who was one of the few players to win both a Super Bowl title and a USFL championship, start for the Pittsburgh Steelers?

    a. 60
    b. 74
    c. 81
    d. 95

19. On two different occasions, former All-American lineman Maurkice Pouncey signed a contract extension with Pittsburgh that made him the highest-paid center in the NFL.

   a. True
   b. False

20. Ray Mansfield played one season for the Philadelphia Eagles before embarking on a long, illustrious career with the Steelers. How many consecutive games did he play for Pittsburgh?

   a. 149
   b. 166
   c. 182
   d. 193

QUIZ ANSWERS

1. B - Kolb's Kowboys

2. A - Turkey

3. A - True

4. B - Epilepsy

5. D - Kendall Simmons

6. B - False

7. A - Moon

8. C - Center

9. B - Dermontti Dawson

10. B - False

11. C - $8,000

12. D - 273

13. C - Carlton Haselrig

14. D - Flag Football

15. A - True

16. B - Steve Courson

17. C - Frank Varrichione

18. C - 81

19. A - True

20. C – 182

DID YOU KNOW?

1. A four-time Super Bowl champion, offensive lineman Jon Kolb was considered one of the strongest men in the NFL. He competed in the second and third editions of the annual World's Strongest Man competitions in the late 1970s and finished fourth in both contests.

2. John Nisby started his pro career with the Steelers in 1957 and was named to a pair of Pro Bowl teams. Besides being one of the first African-American players for the Washington Redskins, which was the last NFL team to integrate, Nisby worked closely with the Rooney family to help provide equal employment opportunities for minorities.

3. Considered one of the key members of the Steelers offensive line, Marvel Smith started 108 games after being selected in the second round of the 2000 NFL Draft. However, injuries in 2007 and 2008 effectively ended his career the following year when Pittsburgh declined to offer Smith a new contract.

4. When he retired in 1990, Mike Webster was the last active NFL player to have been a part of all four Super Bowl-winning teams from the 1970s Steelers. He was also the first former NFL player diagnosed with chronic traumatic encephalopathy, better known as CTE, and he died of a heart attack at the age of 50.

5. Alan Faneca was one of the NFL's top interior linemen and was selected to nine straight Pro Bowls from 2001 through 2009. An excellent pulling guard, Faneca was named to Pittsburgh Steelers All-Time Team and the NFL's 2000s All-Decade Team.

6. A three-time Pro Bowl selection, Will Wolford played the final three seasons of his career with the Steelers. Besides starting 191 NFL games, Wolford was the majority owner/operator of the Louisville Fire of the Arena Football 2. His nephew John Wolford is a backup quarterback with the Los Angeles Rams.

7. Pittsburgh selected Florida offensive tackle Marcus Gilbert in the second round of the 2011 NFL Draft, and he started his pro career on a high note by earning the Steelers Rookie of the Year Award. However, Gilbert was plagued by numerous injuries during his eight-year stint with the franchise and played all 16 games in only two seasons.

8. Max Starks was a mammoth offensive tackle who wore a size 19 shoe and stood 6-foot-8 and weighed 370 pounds. He wore a size 15 shoe as a junior high student and had to borrow shoes from Orlando Magic superstar Shaquille O'Neal. Starks won a pair of Super Bowl rings with Pittsburgh and, although he signed one-year contracts with the San Diego Chargers, St. Louis Rams and Arizona Cardinals, he played just two games with those teams.

9. A United States Army Ranger who was awarded a Bronze Star for valor, offensive tackle Alejandro Villanueva was

the only Steeler to be seen for the national anthem in a 2017 contest against the Chicago Bears. While the rest of the team stayed in the locker room to avoid the national anthem controversy, Villanueva stood in front of the entrance tunnel all alone. The two-time Pro Bowl selection has started 74 games for Pittsburgh since being signed as an undrafted free agent in 2014.

10. One of the most decorated offensive linemen in Steelers' history, Maurkice Pouncey was the 18th overall pick in the 2010 NFL Draft. He was named the franchise Rookie of the Year in his inaugural season and went on to play in eight Pro Bowls through the 2019 season. In a Thursday Night Football matchup against the Cleveland Browns in 2019, Pouncey was involved in a brawl with Myles Garrett that resulted in a three-game suspension.

CHAPTER 7:

THE BACK SEVEN

QUIZ TIME!

1. Which Steeler was drafted in the eighth round of the 1992 NFL Draft and intercepted 6 passes during his rookie season?

    a. Myron Bell
    b. Carnell Lake
    c. Darren Perry
    d. Lee Flowers

2. Joey Porter was a three-time Pro Bowl outside linebacker out of Colorado State who played 122 games for Pittsburgh. How many sacks did he tally during his eight seasons with the Steelers?

    a. 38
    b. 45
    c. 53
    d. 60

3. Mike Wagner, who won four Super Bowl titles with the

Steelers, was the first NAIA All-American to play in the NFL.

   a. True

   b. False

4. Chuck Noll drafted two key members of the Steel Curtain defense in the 1969 NFL Draft. Who were these defensive standouts?

   a. John Baker & Ben McGee

   b. Joe Greene & L.C. Greenwood

   c. Lloyd Voss & Chuck Hinton

   d. Dwight White & Joe Greene

5. I played seven seasons with Pittsburgh and finished my career with 39 interceptions. However, a drug addiction resulted in me losing both of my Super Bowl rings. Who am I?

   a. Mike Wagner

   b. Glen Edwards

   c. Donnie Shell

   d. Ralph Anderson

6. Which former Steelers cornerback practiced law during his final three seasons before becoming a judge in Allegheny County, Pennsylvania?

   a. John Swain

   b. Delton Hall

   c. D.J. Johnson

   d. Dwayne Woodruff

7. Tony Dungy was an undrafted free agent who led the Steelers with 6 interceptions during the 1978 season.

   a. True
   b. False

8. Tagged by Chuck Noll as the fastest Steeler for the first 10 yards, this former Penn State linebacker was a six-time 1st Team All-Pro. He was selected to eight Pro Bowls and was inducted into the Hall of Fame in 1988. Who was this player?

   a. Jack Ham
   b. Loren Toews
   c. Dirt Winston
   d. Andy Russell

9. Troy Polamalu was one of the top defensive backs in league history. Besides being honored as the 2010 NFL Defensive Player of the Year, he also earned eight trips to the Pro Bowl. What year was he elected to the Pro Football Hall of Fame?

   a. 2017
   b. 2018
   c. 2019
   d. 2020

10. What former Steelers safety was named to the NFL 1990s All-Decade Team and the Pittsburgh Steelers All-Time Team?

   a. Lee Flowers
   b. Darren Perry

c. Carnell Lake

d. Travis Davis

11. A member of the famed Steel Curtain defense, Donnie Shell started for the Steelers secondary for 11 consecutive seasons. He retired with the most interceptions by a strong safety in league history and was inducted into the Pro Football Hall of Fame.

a. True

b. False

12. What Steeler cornerback led the NFL with 10 interceptions in 1957 and finished his nine-year career with 52 picks?

a. Jack Butler

b. Russ Craft

c. Gary Glick

d. Howard Hartley

13. David Little played middle linebacker in the NFL for 12 seasons and did not miss a game for several years. How many consecutive games did he play for the Steelers?

a. 78

b. 84

c. 89

d. 93

14. Which Steeler was drafted in the first round of the 1993 NFL Draft after receiving the Jim Thorpe Award and Jack Tatum Trophy as the best college defensive back in the country?

a. Cornell Gowdy

b. Deon Figures

c. Carnell Lake

d. Thomas Everett

15. Rod Woodson is one of the most decorated defensive backs in NFL history. Which of the following awards eluded him during his 17 years in the league?

a. NFL Comeback Player of the Year

b. NFL 100th Anniversary All-Time Team

c. Pittsburgh Steelers All-Time Team

d. NFL Defensive Player of the Year

16. Steelers free safety Minkah Fitzpatrick collected his first NFL interception in 2018 against future Hall of Fame quarterback Tom Brady.

a. True

b. False

17. Linebacker James Harrison was one of the most productive undrafted players in NFL history. His 80.5 career sacks is the most in team history, and in 2008 he achieved a feat that no other undrafted player has ever done. What award did he receive?

a. NFL Rookie of the Year

b. AFC Rookie of the Year

c. Walter Payton Award

d. NFL Defensive Player of the Year

18. Thomas Everett was the safety for the Steelers on how many Super Bowl-winning teams?

a. 0

b. 1

c. 2

d. 3

19. What Steelers defensive back played in 191 of 192 regular-season games and missed only one game due to injury during his 12-year career with four different franchises?

a. Chad Scott

b. Dewayne Washington

c. Donnell Woolford

d. Rod Woodson

20. Hardy Nickerson made five trips to the Pro Bowl and was named the 1997 "Whizzer" White NFL Man of the Year.

a. True

b. False

QUIZ ANSWERS

1. C - Darren Perry

2. D - 60

3. B - False

4. B - Joe Greene & L.C. Greenwood

5. B - Glen Edwards

6. D - Dwayne Woodruff

7. A - True

8. A - Jack Ham

9. D - 2020

10. C - Carnell Lake

11. A - True

12. A - Jack Butler

13. C - 89

14. B - Deon Figures

15. A - NFL Comeback Player of the Year

16. A - True

17. D - NFL Defensive Player of the Year

18. A - 0

19. B - Dewayne Washington

20. A - True

DID YOU KNOW?

1. Legendary cornerback Mel Blount played 14 seasons with the Steelers and helped the franchise win four Super Bowl titles. He was a five-time Pro Bowl selection who was named the NFL Defensive Player of the Year in 1975 after leading the league with 11 interceptions. The Southern University product collected 57 career picks and was inducted into the Pro Football Hall of Fame in 1989.

2. Former Steelers linebacker Ryan Shazier suffers from Alopecia areata, a skin disease that can affect all hair-bearing skin. This autoimmune disorder prevents hair from growing on the body and he was ridiculed during his childhood. However, in 2017, Shazier's hair unexpectedly started growing back.

3. Fred Williamson was a hard-hitting defensive back who played eight seasons of professional football. However, he is better known for his work as an actor once his football career ended. He appeared in the 1996 movie *From Dusk till Dawn* with George Clooney and Quentin Tarantino and acted with Pro Football Hall-of-Famer Jim Brown in the films *Three the Hard Way*, *Take a Hard Ride*, *One Down*, *Original Gangstas* and *On the Edge*. He has also been featured on several television shows, including *M*A*S*H* and *Star Trek*.

4. Considered one of the best outside linebackers in NFL history, Jack Ham spent all 12 years of his professional

career with the Pittsburgh Steelers. Besides being a six-time First-Team All-Pro, he was invited to the Pro Bowl on eight different occasions. Ham was also adept at creating turnovers and finished his career with 53 takeaways, the most ever by a player who was not a defensive back.

5. The Steelers Most Valuable Player in 1987, Mike Merriweather went to three consecutive Pro Bowls in the mid-1980s. He finished fifth in the NFL in 1984 with 15 sacks. Merriweather sat out the entire 1988 season in a contract dispute and was traded to Minnesota. He made history in 1989 when he blocked a punt out of the end zone to become the first player ever to end an overtime game with a safety.

6. One of the few players to win both NFL Defensive Rookie of the Year and NFL Defensive Player of the Year awards, Jack Lambert made nine consecutive trips to the Pro Bowl. He patrolled the middle of the Steelers' ferocious defense for 11 straight years and averaged an amazing 146 tackles a season for a decade. He played college football at Kent State, where he was a teammate of Alabama football coach Nick Saban.

7. Levon Kirkland was a huge inside linebacker for the Steelers who weighed between 275 and 300 pounds during his 11 years in the NFL. Despite his size, he possessed incredible speed and agility. In 1997, he finished with career-highs in both tackles (126) and sacks (5). He was named the Steelers' Most Valuable Player twice and was selected to the NFL 1990s All-Decade Team.

8. A two-time NFL sacks leader, Kevin Greene was one of the league's most feared pass rushers. He played for four teams during his 15-year career, including three seasons with the Steelers. He finished his career with 160 sacks, which ranks third in NFL history. Greene also participated in World Championship Wrestling and was a tag team partner with former professional football player Steve McMichael. However, Greene was forced to stop wrestling when NFL teams started including "no wrestling" clauses in his contracts.

9. A sixth-round draft choice from Fort Valley State University, Greg Lloyd became one of the top players to come out of a historically black university. He earned five trips to the Pro Bowl and was twice selected as the Steelers' Most Valuable Player. An avid mixed martial arts fan, Lloyd has a black belt in Tae Kwon Do. He tallied 54.5 sacks in his career and was named a member of the Pittsburgh Steelers All-Time Team.

10. Considered a reach by NFL draft guru Mel Kiper when Pittsburgh drafted him in the second round in 1989, Carnell Lake was a five-time Pro Bowl selection who was named to the NFL 1990s All-Decade Team. A college linebacker, he finished his career with 16 interceptions and 25 sacks. He is also a member of the Steelers All-Time Team.

CHAPTER 8:

ODDS & ENDS & AWARDS

QUIZ TIME!

1. The Steelers' top draft pick in 1983 was paralyzed in a car crash during his rookie season and finished his six-game career with 2 sacks. Who was he?

    a. Gary Dunn
    b. Steve Furness
    c. Gabriel Rivera
    d. Tom Beasley

2. Cameron Heyward's late father Craig was also a professional football player who rushed for over 4,000 yards and scored 30 touchdowns. His nickname was "Ironhead."

    a. True
    b. False

3. Who was the Steelers starting left defensive end after L.C. Greenwood retired in 1981?

a. Tom Beasley

b. Keith Gary

c. John Goodman

d. John Banaszak

4. Which of these Steelers defensive ends was NOT a first-round pick by the Steelers?

a. Kevin Gary

b. Darryl Sims

c. Aaron Jones

d. Stephon Tuitt

5. I attended the University of North Carolina and was considered one of the top defensive prospects in the 2010 NFL Draft. I was a fifth-round draft pick of the San Diego Chargers who played in 31 games for the Steelers over two seasons. Who am I?

a. Cam Thomas

b. Evander Hood

c. Casey Hampton

d. Steve McLendon

6. Roy Gerela is the only kicker to win the Steelers MVP Award.

a. True

b. False

7. Which one of the following players was NOT named to the Pittsburgh Steelers All-Time Team?

a. Jack Butler

b. Ernie Holmes

c. Andy Russell

d. Dwight White

8. Only four teams were founded before the Steelers were founded in 1933. Which of the following teams was NOT established before the Pittsburgh franchise?

   a. Green Bay Packers

   b. Chicago Bears

   c. New York Giants

   d. Cleveland Browns

9. The Pittsburgh Steelers won the Super Bowl in 1979, and the Pittsburgh Pirates won the World Series that same year.

   a. True

   b. False

10. Mean Joe Greene was named NFL Defensive Player of the Year twice in three seasons. What years did he win this award?

    a. 1971 & 1973

    b. 1972 & 1974

    c. 1975 & 1977

    d. 1978 & 1980

11. Pittsburgh drafted a whopping nine future Hall of Fame players in a span of five years from 1969 to 1974. Which of the following players were never inducted into the Pro Football Hall of Fame?

    a. Mel Blount

    b. Jack Butler

c. Bobby Layne

d. L.C. Greenwood

12. In 1975, the Steelers put together a record-setting winning streak en route to their first Super Bowl title. How many consecutive games did Pittsburgh win?

a. 9

b. 10

c. 11

d. 13

13. The Pittsburgh Steelers' only winless season came in 1944 when the franchise was forced to merge with another team due to World War II. What team did the Steelers merge with?

a. New York Giants

b. Baltimore Colts

c. Chicago Cardinals

d. Philadelphia Eagles

14. Which of these players did NOT wear the #75 Jersey?

a. George Hays

b. Joe Greene

c. Ken Kortas

d. Marvel Smith

15. The Pittsburgh franchise advanced to the playoffs twice before the AFL merged with the NFL.

a. True

b. False

16. Which one of the following players has made the most Pro Bowl appearances for the Steelers?

    a. Joe Greene
    b. Lynn Swann
    c. Jack Ham
    d. Franco Harris

17. The Steelers' main team colors have been black and gold except for one season. What other team colors have the Steelers worn?

    a. Black and White
    b. Green and White
    c. Black and Grey
    d. Gold and White

18. I finished my career with 73.5 sacks and led the Steelers in sacks on six different occasions. I was also voted to the Pro Bowl six times and was on four Super Bowl championship teams. Who am I?

    a. Ernie Holmes
    b. Dwight White
    c. L.C. Greenwood
    d. John Banaszak

19. The Steelers had a roster in 1979 that consisted of no players that had suited up for another NFL squad.

    a. True
    b. False

20. Who posted a 3-6-2 record in 1933 as the first coach in the history of the Pittsburgh franchise?

a. Forrest Douds
b. Joe Bach
c. John McNally
d. Walt Kiesling

QUIZ ANSWERS

1. C - Gabriel Rivera

2. A - True

3. C - John Goodman

4. D - Stephon Tuitt

5. A - Cam Thomas

6. B - False

7. B - Ernie Holmes

8. D – Cleveland Browns

9. A - True

10. B - 1972 & 1974

11. D - L.C. Greenwood

12. C - 11

13. C - Chicago Cardinals

14. D - Marvel Smith

15. A - True

16. A - Joe Greene

17. B - Green and White

18. C - L.C. Greenwood

19. A - True

20. A - Forrest Douds

DID YOU KNOW?

1. Dwight White won four Super Bowl titles with the Steelers and finished his career with 46 sacks. He lost 20 pounds due to pneumonia and spent most of the week leading up to Super Bowl IX in the hospital. He is credited with scoring the first points in the franchise's Super Bowl history when he sacked Minnesota's Fran Tarkenton in the end zone for a safety.

2. One of the most dominant defensive players in NFL history, Mean Joe Greene was the centerpiece of a Steeler defense that led the franchise to four Super Bowl wins in the 1970s. He was honored as the NFL Defensive Rookie of the Year in 1969 despite the team finishing with a dismal 1-13 record. He was inducted into both the College Football Hall of Fame and the Pro Football Hall of Fame. Greene also starred in an iconic Coca-Cola commercial where he said, "Hey kid, catch!" and tossed his jersey to a little boy after a game.

3. A German immigrant who fought in World War II, Ernie Stautner played 13 seasons for the Steelers and was selected to the Pro Bowl nine times. He was the first player to have his jersey retired by the franchise. He won two Super Bowls as a defensive coach for the Dallas Cowboys and was also a head coach in the Arena Football League and NFL Europe.

4. Pittsburgh selected Cameron Heyward with the 31st overall pick in the 2011 NFL Draft. He was a two-time First-Team All-Pro selection and recorded 54 sacks over his first nine seasons. He was fined by the league during the NFL 2015 Breast Cancer Awareness campaign for displaying his father's nickname in eye black even though his dad was a former pro football player who died of cancer.

5. A member of The Church of Jesus Christ of Latter-day Saints, Brett Keisel played his entire 13-year career with the Steelers. He racked up 30 sacks and rambled 79 yards after picking off an errant pass against the Tampa Bay Buccaneers. He has raised more than $725,000 with his annual "Shear the Beard Event" that benefits the Children's Hospital of Pittsburgh of UPMC.

6. Chuck Noll was the architect of the 1970s Steelers dynasty that won back-to-back Super Bowls on two different occasions. He was a two-way player for the Cleveland Browns, where he was a member of two NFL Championship squads. He was the 14th head coach in franchise history and his streak of coaching the same team for 23 years is second only to Tom Landry's 29 years with the Cowboys among coaches who only coached one franchise in their career.

7. Gary Anderson was the first South African to play in the NFL, where he played for 23 seasons. He is the all-time leading scorer for Pittsburgh and is a member of the Steelers All-Time Team. He became the first kicker in

league history to convert every point after touchdown and field goal in a season in 1998. He made four trips to the Pro Bowl and his 538 career field goals ranks third in NFL history.

8. In 2019, T.J. Watt became the first defensive player to win the Pittsburgh Steelers Most Valuable Player Award since safety Troy Polamalu took home the trophy in 2010. Receiver Antonio Brown has won the award four times, while defensive back Rod Woodson, receiver Hines Ward and running back Jerome Bettis each won the award on three different occasions.

9. The Steelers' 50th overall selection in the 1994 NFL Draft, Brentson Buckner tallied 31 sacks and 2 interceptions during his 12 seasons in the league. While at Clemson, he had a 1,220-pound lift on a leg slide that set a school record. He blocked several field goals during his career with the Steelers, Cincinnati Bengals, San Francisco 49ers and Carolina Panthers.

10. A Steeler special teams' standout his first two seasons, Jason Gildon was a third-round draft choice who developed into a strong pass rusher. He finished his career with 80 sacks and a trio of defensive touchdowns. A three-time Pro Bowl selection, he is the older half-brother of defensive end Larry Birdine, who was once on the Tennessee Titans' practice squad.

CHAPTER 9:

NICKNAMES

QUIZ TIME!

1. Dwight White was a high-intensity player who retired from the NFL after a 10-year career with the Steelers. What was his nickname?

    a. Wolverine

    b. Mad Dog

    c. Badger

    d. Bronco

2. Which Pittsburgh third-string quarterback was called "Jefferson Street" by his teammates?

    a. Cliff Stoudt

    b. Mike Tomczak

    c. Terry Hanratty

    d. Joe Gilliam

3. Which undrafted Steeler middle linebacker was nicknamed "Potsie" by his parents because he had a potbelly as a kid?

a. Larry Foote

b. Kendrell Bell

c. James Farrior

d. Lawrence Timmons

4. Steelers' founder Art Rooney Sr. was also an Olympic qualifying boxer who was called the Chief.

a. True

b. False

5. Nicknamed "Count Dracula in Cleats," I was drafted in the second round in 1974 and went to the Pro Bowl nine consecutive seasons. Who am I?

a. Loren Toews

b. Jack Lambert

c. Henry Davis

d. Andy Russell

6. Pittsburgh released outside linebacker James Harrison three times before he finally made the roster. He rewarded the team by winning the NFL Defensive Player of the Year in 2008. What was his nickname?

a. Houdini

b. Silverback

c. Baby Bull

d. Superman

7. Fred Williamson was a hard-hitting defensive back who played one season for the Steelers before going to Hollywood to become an actor. What nickname did an opposing coach give him during his first training camp?

a. The Hammer

b. Crusher

c. 911

d. Ball Hawk

8. Jerome Bettis resurrected his career with Pittsburgh and was called "The Train" while leading the Steelers to a win in Super Bowl XL.

   a. True

   b. False

9. A ferocious hitter who was one of the NFL's most intelligent players to play linebacker, both his nickname and his fan club was called "Dobre Shunka." What was his name?

   a. Jack Ham

   b. Chuck Allen

   c. Robin Cole

   d. Dirt Winston

10. Casey Hampton was a 325-pound nose tackle who went to five Pro Bowls as a member of the Steelers. What was his nickname?

   a. The Big Cheese

   b. Snickerdoodle

   c. The Big Snack

   d. Pit Bull

11. An intense linebacker whose nickname was "Peezy," Joey Porter forced 25 fumbles during his career.

a. True

b. False

12. Three Rivers Stadium was one of the toughest venues for opposing teams and Pittsburgh posted a 69-13 record there in the 1970s. What was the nickname of this old stadium?

a. House of Horrors

b. The Blast Furnace

c. The Steel Pit

d. The Barnyard

13. In 1978, Hall of Fame running back Earl Campbell broke a long run before getting drilled by Steelers strong safety Donnie Shell. The hit broke several of Campbell's ribs and Shell was given a new nickname. What was he called?

a. The Torpedo

b. The Missile

c. Atom Bomb

d. The Enforcer

14. After he won the MVP award in the XFL, the Steelers signed quarterback Tommy Maddox, who rallied the team to a division title after an 0-2 start. Because of his aerial prowess, what nickname was he given?

a. Mad Maddox

b. Man of Steel

c. Tommy Gun

d. Brunette Bomber

15. Hines "Papa Smurf" Ward was an all-around wide receiver

who was called "tougher than woodpecker lips" by a teammate.

a. True
b. False

16. Although the Steelers defense in the 1970s was known as the Steel Curtain, the franchise has also been called another popular name. What is this other nickname?

a. Dirty Dozen
b. Black & Gold Army
c. Steel Battalion
d. Men of Steel

17. It is rare for cities to adopt a nickname based on its football team, but Pittsburgh fans did just that in the 1990s due to a new defensive scheme that caused chaos for opposing teams. What nickname did Steeler fans call their city?

a. Blitzburgh
b. Blitz Town
c. Blitzville
d. Pittblitz

18. What Hall of Fame Steeler was called the "Tasmanian Devil" due to his versatility and playmaking skills?

a. Mel Blount
b. Donnie Shell
c. Troy Polamalu
d. Rod Woodson

19. Ben Roethlisberger was called "Big Ben" after the big clock tower at the north side of Westminster Palace?

a. True

b. False

20. Which Pittsburgh legend shares the same nickname as Mike Tyson?

a. Franco Harris

b. Marion Motley

c. Dermontti Dawson

d. Mike Webster

QUIZ ANSWERS

1. B - Mad Dog

2. D - Joe Gilliam

3. C - James Farrior

4. A - True

5. B - Jack Lambert

6. B - Silverback

7. A - The Hammer

8. B - False

9. A - Jack Ham

10. C - The Big Snack

11. A - True

12. B - The Blast Furnace

13. A - The Torpedo

14. C - Tommy Gun

15. A - True

16. D - Men of Steel

17. A - Blitzburgh

18. C - Troy Polamalu

19. A - True

20. D - Mike Webster

DID YOU KNOW?

1. Terry Bradshaw was the NFL's top overall pick in 1970 and he struggled mightily in his first few seasons. Known as the "Blonde Bomber," he developed into a four-time Super Bowl champion with a pair of Super Bowl MVP trophies. He was a perfect 4-0 in the Super Bowl and was also the first quarterback to win three and then four Super Bowl rings.

2. Considered one of the best talent evaluators in the history of the NFL, Chuck Noll won two NFL Championships as a player and four Super Bowl titles as the head coach of the Steelers. He was given his nickname, Emperor Chaz, by Pittsburgh sportscaster Myron Cope. Noll retired from playing professional football at the age of 27 to begin his coaching career.

3. "Mean Joe" Greene was one of the most dominant defensive linemen to ever play in the NFL. He anchored the legendary Steel Curtain defense that propelled the franchise to four Vince Lombardi trophies. A freakish 6'4", 275-pounder who possessed a unique combination of speed and power, Greene was a big-play artist who caused chaos in opposing backfields.

4. Acquired in a trade in 1996, Jerome Bettis arrived in Pittsburgh with a lot of baggage. However, "The Bus" established himself as one of the league's premier running

backs with the Steelers. He was honored as the NFL Comeback Player of the Year in his first season with Pittsburgh and was invited to the Pro Bowl six times. Bettis finished his career with 13,662 yards and 91 touchdowns and was inducted into the Pro Football Hall of Fame in 2015.

5. The name of the legendary "Steel Curtain" defense came as a result of a contest. Several people submitted the new nickname and a random drawing was held to determine the winner. The name was based on the popular phrase, "Iron Curtain," favored by Winston Churchill to describe the isolation of the Soviet Union. Although the entire defensive squad was given the nickname, many believe the moniker was for the defensive line that featured Mean Joe Greene, Dwight White, L.C. Greenwood and Ernie Holmes.

6. Kordell Stewart was a jack-of-all-trades player who earned the nickname "Slash" as a rookie backup quarterback because of his receiving skills. Whether he was catching touchdown passes or lining up at quarterback or running back, Stewart was an electric athlete. He was named the AFC Offensive Player of the Year in 2001 and earned his only trip to the Pro Bowl. He finished his career with 14,746 passing yards, 2,874 rushing yards and 120 total touchdowns (77 passing, 38 rushing and five receiving).

7. One of the top defensive backs ever to step on an NFL field, Rod Woodson was inducted into the Pro Football Hall of Fame in 2009. He intercepted 71 passes during his

17 seasons in the league, which ranks third in NFL history. The 1993 NFL Defensive Player of the Year returned 12 interceptions for touchdowns and recovered an NFL-record 32 fumbles. He was elected to the College Football Hall of Fame in 2016.

8. A halfback who led the NFL in rushing twice, Byron "Whizzer" White played three seasons in the NFL before becoming a judge. He signed one of the largest contracts in professional football when Pittsburgh signed him to a $15,000 deal in 1938, which was equivalent to $270,000 in 2019 dollars. He served as an intelligence officer in World War II and retired from football after the war to pursue his law degree.

9. A dynamic offensive lineman who played in 170 consecutive games for the Steelers, Dermontti Dawson was gifted with two nicknames. He was called Ned Flanders, a character on the Simpsons animated television series, because of his laidback demeanor off the field. But on the field, he was nicknamed "Dirt" because of his ability to grind defenders into the ground. He earned seven trips to the Pro Bowl and was inducted into the Pro Football Hall of Fame in 2012.

10. John McNally was one of the few players who blessed himself with his own nickname. He played semi-pro football in 1922 to earn extra money, but to protect his college eligibility he used the name Johnny Blood. He won four NFL Championships as a player with Green Bay Packers and was named to the National Football League

1930s All-Decade Team. McNally played 14 seasons in the NFL and was elected to the Pro Football Hall of Fame as a charter member in 1963.

CHAPTER 10:

ALMA MATERS

QUIZ TIME!

1. I was an All-American punt returner at Central Michigan who caught more passes than any other NFL player during my first nine years of professional football. Who am I?

   a. Louis Lipps
   b. Antonio Brown
   c. John Stallworth
   d. Mike Wallace

2. Ben Roethlisberger threw for over 5,000 yards during his third season at Miami University in Ohio.

   a. True
   b. False

3. Greg Lloyd was a three-time Defensive MVP in college who was the SIAC Player of the Year and a first-team Sheridan All-American selection his senior year. What historical black university did he attend?

a. Alcorn State

b. Florida A&M

c. Fort Valley State

d. South Carolina State

4. Which of the following Steelers did NOT play college football at Penn State?

a. Jack Ham

b. Franco Harris

c. Leroy Thompson

d. Ronnie Shanklin

5. Which Steelers offensive lineman went to LSU and started the final 36 games of his college career while amassing 210 pancake blocks?

a. Alan Faneca

b. J. W. Goree

c. George Tarasovic

d. Jerald Hawkins

6. Receivers Hines Ward, Andre Hastings and Fred Gibson all played college football for the Georgia Bulldogs?

a. True

b. False

7. Steeler T.J. Watt and his two brothers, J.J. and Derek, all became NFL players and attended the same college. Where did they go to school?

a. Illinois

b. Wisconsin

c. Oregon

d. Michigan

8. During my first two years at Syracuse, I played on the soccer team and led my team in goals one season before I turned my focus to football. Who am I?

   a. Matt Bahr

   b. Jeff Reed

   c. Gary Anderson

   d. Roy Gerela

9. Which future Hall-of-Famer quit football after his freshman year in high school, but resumed playing in his junior year and earned a scholarship to the University of Kentucky?

   a. George Blanda

   b. Irv Goode

   c. Vito "Babe" Parilli

   d. Dermontti Dawson

10. Linebacker Joey Porter registered 20 career sacks in college and was a four-time Pro Bowl selection. What college did he attend?

    a. Howard University

    b. Colorado State

    c. Grambling State

    d. Ohio University

11. Which of the following Steelers did NOT play college football at Vanderbilt?

a. Mark Malone

b. Will Wolford

c. Ed Smith

d. Barry Burton

12. Kimo von Oelhoffen graduated from a high school without a football team and played at the University of Hawaii and Walla Walla Community College before transferring to Boise State.

a. True

b. False

13. Mean Joe Greene's options for playing college football in Texas were limited due to segregation in the Southwest Conference. What college did he attend?

a. Abilene Christian

b. University of North Texas

c. Stephen F. Austin

d. East Texas State

14. The Pacific Tigers disbanded their football team in 1995 for financial reasons. Which of the following Steelers played college football at the University of Pacific?

a. Bobby Layne

b. Ray Mansfield

c. Mike Merriweather

d. Rashard Mendenhall

15. What Steeler Hall-of-Famer attended St. Mary's, a private Catholic college in California, where the basketball team is more popular than the football team?

a. Chuck Noll

b. Terry Bradshaw

c. John Stallworth

d. John Henry Johnson

16. Kent State University has produced three Steelers who have won a combined 10 Super Bowl rings.

a. True

b. False

17. One of the four members of Pittsburgh's famous Steel Curtain, L.C. Greenwood played football at a small college whose football team was called the Golden Lions. What college did he attend?

a. Arkansas-Pine Bluff

b. Spelman College

c. Tarleton State

d. North Carolina A&T

18. What Steeler Hall-of-Famer attended the University of St. Thomas, a Division III school in Minnesota?

a. Jack Butler

b. Walt Kiesling

c. Bill Dudley

d. Dan Rooney

19. John Stallworth earned a Bachelor of Science degree in Business Administration and an MBA with a concentration in Finance from Alabama A&M University.

a. True

b. False

20. Which of the following Steelers did NOT play college football at Winston-Salem State University?

    a. Yancey Thigpen

    b. Donald Evans

    c. Marion Motley

    d. Richard Huntley

QUIZ ANSWERS

1. B - Antonio Brown

2. B - False

3. C - Fort Valley State

4. D - Ronnie Shanklin

5. A - Alan Faneca

6. A - True

7. B - Wisconsin

8. C - Gary Anderson

9. D - Dermontti Dawson

10. B - Colorado State

11. A - Mark Malone

12. A - True

13. B - University of North Texas

14. C - Mike Merriweather

15. D - John Henry Johnson

16. B - False

17. A - Arkansas-Pine Bluff

18. B - Walt Kiesling

19. A - True

20. C - Marion Motley

DID YOU KNOW?

1. Steelers' founder Art Rooney and his son, Dan Rooney, both attended Duquesne University, a private Catholic university in Pittsburgh. Art also spent time at Temple University on an athletic scholarship. In 1933, Duquesne named its football field after Art. Dan graduated from Duquesne with a degree in accounting. Running back Mike Basrak, who was drafted by the franchise in 1937, also attended Duquesne.

2. Ohio State University has produced the most first-round draft picks for the Steelers. Running back Bob Ferguson, wide receiver Santonio Holmes, defensive end Cameron Heyward and linebacker Ryan Shazier all competed for the Buckeyes. Holmes was chosen the MVP of Super Bowl XLIII after a game-winning touchdown catch in the final seconds. Heyward has been selected to three Pro Bowls during his first nine seasons, while Shazier was a two-time Pro Bowl selection before his career was cut short due to a spinal injury.

3. Pittsburgh has only drafted one player from Alabama A&M, but he was Hall-of-Famer John Stallworth. The Alabama native was the 82nd player taken in the 1974 NFL Draft and went on to win four Super Bowls in a 14-year career. The three-time Pro Bowl selection caught 537 passes for 8,723 yards and 63 touchdowns. Stallworth, who is a part-owner of the Steelers, is one of only two players to have their jerseys retired by Alabama A&M.

4. Lane College in Jackson, Tennessee has an enrollment of fewer than 2,000 students, but has produced four NFL players. Jacoby Jones played only four games with the Steelers in 2015 but enjoyed an effective career as a punt returner for several teams. He retired with 203 receptions and over 7,000 return yards.

5. Historical black colleges and universities (HBCU) have been the training ground for numerous Pro Football Hall-of-Famers, including four Steelers. Mel Blount (Southern), Marion Motley (South Carolina State), John Stallworth (Alabama A&M) and Donnie Shell (South Carolina State) all honed their skills at HBCU schools. Blount and Shell played seven seasons together in the Pittsburgh secondary and combined for 108 career interceptions. Motley played just one season for the Black and Gold, while Stallworth racked up 63 receiving touchdowns.

6. A whopping 11 players from the University of North Texas have been drafted by the Steelers, including Hall of Fame defensive lineman Joe Greene. Although most of the players from the Mean Green did not contribute much to the franchise, Green became the anchor of the Steel Curtain defense and one of the top players to ever play in the NFL. Halfback Abner Haynes scored 66 combined rushing and receiving touchdowns – though none for the Steelers – and wide receiver Ron Shanklin caught 24 touchdown passes.

7. Pittsburgh has recruited well in the Big 12 (formerly Southwest Conference) and has found numerous gems

from Baylor University. Some of the most productive Bears to suit up for the Steelers includes defensive Thomas Everett, running backs Walter Abercrombie and Frank Pollard, tight end Jack Russell and halfback Billy Patterson.

8. The Penn State Nittany Lions have been one of the preferred pipelines for the Steelers in their quest for talented players. Besides Hall-of-Famers Jack Ham and Franco Harris, other productive players from Penn State were tight end Jesse James, running back Leroy Thompson, defensive tackle Tim Johnson, running back Dick Hoak and fullback Fran Rogel.

9. The Steelers have not recruited from any school more than the University of Pittsburgh. Although the franchise struck out by not drafting Panthers quarterback Dan Marino, the Steelers have selected nearly 50 players from Pitt. However, running back James Conner and quarterback Alex Van Pelt are the only players who had any type of production.

10. In the early years of the franchise, Pittsburgh favored drafting players from Notre Dame due to Art Rooney's Catholic background. However, from 2014 to 2020, the Steelers only drafted two players from South Bend. The first draft pick in team history was used to select Fighting Irish running back William "Bill" Shakespeare, who opted not to play professional football. Other notable players from Notre Dame include linebacker Myron Pottios, offensive tackle Frank Varrichione, halfback Johnny

Lattner, running back Rocky Bleier, quarterback Terry Hanratty, defensive end Stephon Tuitt and wide receiver Chase Claypool.

CHAPTER 11:

IN THE DRAFT ROOM

QUIZ TIME!

1. Who was the last player that the Steelers drafted with the top overall pick in the NFL draft?

    a. Plaxico Burress

    b. Terry Bradshaw

    c. Bill Dudley

    d. J.T. Thomas

2. What year did the Steelers draft four future Hall-of-Famers in the same draft?

    a. 1970

    b. 1971

    c. 1974

    d. 1975

3. William "Bill" Shakespeare was the first player ever drafted by the Pittsburgh franchise.

    a. True

    b. False

4. Since 1936, which college has had the most players drafted by the Steelers?

    a. Notre Dame
    b. Penn State
    c. University of Pittsburgh
    d. University of Florida

5. For three consecutive drafts from 2017-2019, the Steelers drafted two players from the same college. Which of the following duos were not drafted in the same year?

    a. Devin Bush Jr. & Zach Gentry
    b. Mason Rudolph & James Washington
    c. Cameron Sutton & Josh Dobbs
    d. Marcus Gilbert & Maurkice Pouncey

6. How many players have the Steelers drafted in the first round who have been inducted into the Pro Football Hall of Fame?

    a. 5
    b. 8
    c. 10
    d. 12

7. Pittsburgh drafted four players from the University of Pittsburgh in both the 1956 and 1957 NFL drafts.

    a. True
    b. False

8. Since the 2005 NFL Draft, the Steelers have selected a wide receiver in every draft except one. What was the year that Pittsburgh did NOT draft a wide receiver?

a. 2007

b. 2018

c. 2015

d. 2011

9. What Citadel cornerback did the Steelers select in the fourth round of the 2011 NFL Draft?

a. Curtis Brown

b. Crezdon Butler

c. Cortez Allen

d. Terrence Frederick

10. In 1990, Pittsburgh used their first-round draft pick to select a tight end from Liberty University. Who was the player drafted by the Steelers?

a. Adrian Cooper

b. Eric Green

c. Bruce McGonnigal

d. Mike Hinnant

11. The Steelers drafted a pair of Hall of Fame quarterbacks in the 1950s but neither made an impact with the franchise before finding success with other organizations. Who were they?

a. Johnny Unitas & Len Dawson

b. Len Dawson & Earl Morrall

c. Johnny Unitas & Len Dawson

d. Bill Dudley & Earl Morrall

12. Rocky Bleier rushed for over 3,800 yards and won four

Super Bowl rings despite being the 417th player picked in 1968.

a. True

b. False

13. Pittsburgh drafted nine future Hall-of-Famers from 1969 to 1974. In what year in that span did the Steelers fail to draft a Hall of Fame player?

a. 1969

b. 1970

c. 1971

d. 1973

14. The Steelers have drafted three University of Florida players in the first round. Which of the following players was NOT a first-round draft pick?

a. Paul Duhart

b. Huey Richardson

c. Marcus Gilbert

d. Maurkice Pouncey

15. Pittsburgh is the only team in NFL history to have four first-round picks in one draft.

a. True

b. False

16. Terry Bradshaw was the NFL's top overall pick in 1970. Which college did he attend?

a. LSU

b. Arkansas-Pine Bluff

c. Louisiana at Lafayette

d. Louisiana Tech

17. From 2017 to 2020, the Steelers drafted two players from the same college.

    a. True

    b. False

18. Chuck Noll played college football at Dayton before playing seven seasons with the Cleveland Browns. What round was he selected in the 1953 NFL Draft?

    a. 9

    b. 11

    c. 20

    d. 15

19. The Steelers selected wide receivers with their first pick in back-to-back drafts only once in their history. Who were these first-round draft picks?

    a. Troy Edwards & Plaxico Burress

    b. Emmanuel Sanders & Antonio Brown

    c. Santonio Holmes & Limas Sweed

    d. Antwaan Randle El & Santonio Holmes

20. Casey Hampton was drafted in the first round by the Steelers in 2001 after a dominating career at what Big 12 school?

    a. Baylor

    b. Oklahoma

    c. Oklahoma State

    d. Texas

QUIZ ANSWERS

1. B - Terry Bradshaw

2. C - 1974

3. A - True

4. C - University of Pittsburgh

5. D - Marcus Gilbert & Maurkice Pouncey

6. B - 8

7. A - True

8. D - 2011

9. C - Cortez Allen

10. B - Eric Green

11. A - Johnny Unitas & Len Dawson

12. A - True

13. D - 1973

14. C - Marcus Gilbert

15. B - False

16. D - Louisiana Tech

17. A - True

18. C - 20

19. A - Troy Edwards & Plaxico Burress

20. D – Texas

DID YOU KNOW?

1. In 2020, the Pittsburgh drafted Notre Dame wide receiver Chase Claypool with the 49th overall pick in the second round. The 2020 NFL Draft was the first time the Steelers did not have a first-round draft choice since 1967, when the franchise selected San Diego State running back Don Shy with the 35th pick. The franchise also did not have a first-rounder in seven other seasons, including three times in the 1960s, twice in the 1950s, and once both in the 1940s and 1930s.

2. Chuck Noll and the Steelers made history in 1974 by drafting four future Hall-of-Famers despite not having a third-round pick. Pittsburgh drafted wide receiver Lynn Swann, linebacker Jack Lambert, wide receiver John Stallworth, defensive back Jimmy Allen and center Mike Webster with their first five picks. The Steelers also signed safety Donnie Shell as an undrafted free agent that same year. Shell was elected to the Pro Football Hall of Fame in 2020 to become the fifth rookie on the Steelers 1974 roster to receive a Gold Jacket.

3. The Steelers have historically had more hits than misses with their first-round selections. Although Pittsburgh missed on their very first draft pick in franchise history when Notre Dame back William "Bill" Shakespeare opted for a business career, the Steelers had only one first-round draft bust from 1995 to 2019. In 1996, Pittsburgh selected

North Carolina A&T offensive tackle Jamain Stephens with the 29th pick. However, Smith played in only 40 games with the team over three unimpressive seasons.

4. Notre Dame fullback Rocky Bleier was the 417th player selected in the 1968 NFL Draft and one of the Steelers' most productive late-round picks in team history. Bleier, who lost part of his foot during the Vietnam War, won four Super Bowls with Pittsburgh and rushed for 3,865 yards and 23 touchdowns over 11 seasons.

5. The Steelers' draft success from 1969 to 1974 is unmatched in NFL history. Chuck Noll selected University of North Texas defensive tackle Joe Greene with the fourth pick in the 1969 NFL Draft. Over the next six years, the Steelers drafted a future Hall of Fame player in every draft except for 1973. Besides Greene, Noll selected legendary players Terry Bradshaw (1970), Mel Blount (1970), Jack Ham (1971), Franco Harris (1972), Lynn Swann (1974), Jack Lambert (1974), John Stallworth (1974) and Mike Webster (1974). Another future Hall-of-Famer, Donnie Shell, was signed as an undrafted free agent in 1974.

6. In a span of three years, Pittsburgh drafted a pair of Hall of Fame quarterbacks that they let slip through their fingers. The Steelers drafted Johnny Unitas in the ninth round but released him before the 1955 season started. He went on to throw for over 40,000 yards and 290 touchdowns and is considered one of the greatest quarterbacks of all-time. Two years later, in 1957, Pittsburgh selected Len Dawson with the fifth overall pick. However, he was traded to the

Cleveland Browns in 1959 after the Steelers acquired another Hall of Fame quarterback, Bobby Layne, from the Detroit Lions. Dawson finished his career with 28,711 passing yards and 239 touchdown passes.

7. Former broadcaster and Las Vegas Raiders general manager Mike Mayock was drafted by the Steelers in the 10th round of the 1981 NFL Draft. Although he was released by the franchise, he played one game in the Canadian Football League with the Toronto Argonauts and he joined the New York Giants for two seasons before retiring. Before joining the Raiders organization, Mayock was a successful broadcaster with the NFL Network.

8. In 1984, the Steelers were awarded three picks in the USFL Supplemental Draft. Pittsburgh selected Indiana wide receiver Duane Gunn with the 23rd pick, Michigan center Tom Dixon with the 52nd pick and Arkansas offensive tackle Phillip Boren with the 79th pick. Unfortunately, none of the three ever played a game in the NFL.

9. Pittsburgh selected Dayton wide receiver Kelvin Kirk with the 487th pick of the 1976 NFL Draft. Kirk was the final selection of the draft and was the first person to be given the title, Mr. Irrelevant. He was released by the Steelers but he played seven seasons in the Canadian Football League with four different teams. He finished his pro football career with 153 receptions and 20 total touchdowns.

10. The Steelers have drafted two players from the same college in four consecutive drafts from 2017 to 2020 under

general manager Kevin Colbert. The trend began in 2017 when a pair of Tennessee Volunteers were drafted, defensive back Cameron Sutton and quarterback Joshua Dobbs. The following season, Oklahoma State standouts James Washington and Mason Rudolph were selected. In 2019, Pittsburgh took the Michigan duo of Devin Bush and Zack Gentry and followed that up by taking Maryland teammates Anthony McFarland and Antoine Brooks in the 2020 NFL Draft.

CHAPTER 12:

THE TRADING POST

QUIZ TIME!

1. What Super Bowl MVP was traded to the New York Jets one season after winning a Super Bowl ring?

   a. Mike Wallace

   b. Luis Lipps

   c. Santonio Holmes

   d. Plaxico Burress

2. The Steelers acquired a sixth-round draft pick from the Arizona Cardinals that was used to draft Antonio Brown.

   a. True

   b. False

3. What Pittsburgh punter was traded to the New York Giants for a conditional seventh-round pick in the 2016 NFL Draft after losing a punting competition to Jordan Berry?

   a. Drew Butler

   b. Brad Wing

c. Daniel Sepulveda

d. Jeremy Kapinos

4. I was a second-round draft pick of the San Francisco 49ers who was packaged with a 2018 fifth-rounder in 2017 and traded to the Steelers for a 2018 fourth-round selection. Who am I?

a. Jesse James

b. Ryan Switzer

c. Matt Feiler

d. Vance McDonald

5. Pittsburgh traded wide receiver Martavis Bryant to the Oakland Raiders during the 2018 draft for a third-round pick. The Steelers used the 79th pick to move up three spots to select which quarterback?

a. Joshua Dobbs

b. Landry Jones

c. Mason Rudolph

d. Devlin Hodges

6. The Steelers traded Antonio Brown to the Oakland Raiders for a pair of draft picks during the 2019 NFL Draft. Which two players did Pittsburgh draft with the picks acquired from the Raiders?

a. Diontae Johnson & Zach Gentry

b. Justin Layne & Benny Snell Jr.

c. Devin Bush & Sutton Smith

d. Marcus Allen & Chukwuma Okorafor

7. Due to the career-ending injury to Ryan Shazier, Pittsburgh traded two first-round draft picks in the 2019 NFL Draft to move up 10 spots to draft Michigan linebacker Devin Bush.

   a. True
   b. False

8. The Steelers and the Miami Dolphins completed a blockbuster trade in 2019 in which five draft picks and a player were swapped. Who was the player who was traded to Pittsburgh?

   a. James Conner
   b. Jaylen Samuels
   c. Terrell Edmunds
   d. Minkah Fitzpatrick

9. When Pittsburgh and the Cleveland Browns exchanged draft picks during the 2013 NFL Draft, it was the first time in decades that the two teams were involved in a transaction. Before this exchange, when was the last time these two rivals traded players or draft picks?

   a. June 7, 1972
   b. April 29, 1970
   c. May 14, 1968
   d. August 3, 1966

10. The Steelers were focused on rebuilding their defense in 2001 when they made several trades during the draft. Which two players did Pittsburgh select with the 19th and 39th picks?

a. Kendrick Clancy & Hank Poteat

b. Casey Hampton & Kendrell Bell

c. Troy Polamalu & Alonzo Jackson

d. Scott Shields & Joey Porter

11. In the 2010 NFL Draft, the Tampa Bay Buccaneers traded a quarterback to the Steelers for a seventh-round draft pick. Which player was traded to Pittsburgh?

a. Charlie Batch

b. Dennis Dixon

c. Landry Jones

d. Byron Leftwich

12. Pittsburgh traded their No. 1 draft pick away five times, and their No. 2 pick four times between 1958 and 1965.

a. True

b. False

13. Which Steeler played four seasons with the franchise and won two Super Bowls before leaving as a free agent, and then getting traded back to Pittsburgh after one season?

a. James Farrior

b. Anthony Smith

c. Bryant McFadden

d. Dewayne Washington

14. Which ultra-talented player did the Steelers covet so much in the 2003 NFL Draft that they traded three draft picks to the Kansas City Chiefs to move up 11 spots to the 16th pick?

a. Plaxico Burress

b. Troy Polamalu

c. Casey Hampton

d. Ben Roethlisberger

15. What little-known cornerback did the Steelers select in the 2004 NFL Draft after sending two draft picks to the Indianapolis Colts to move up six spots?

a. Ike Taylor

b. Chris Hope

c. Anthony Smith

d. Ricardo Colclough

16. Chuck Noll preferred to build a team from the draft and rarely made trades. However, he broke with tradition in 1973 and sent a third-round pick to the Oakland Raiders for defensive tackle Tom Keating.

a. True

b. False

17. In one of the most lopsided trades in NFL history, the Steelers acquired a future Hall-of-Famer and a third-round pick in 1996 from the St. Louis Rams for a second-round pick and a fourth-rounder. Which player did Pittsburgh get from the Rams?

a. Bam Morris

b. Joey Porter

c. Jerome Bettis

d. Kordell Stewart

18. What player did the Steelers draft with the second-round selection they received from the New York Jets for three draft picks during the 1998 NFL Draft?

    a. Alan Faneca

    b. Jeremy Staat

    c. Chris Conrad

    d. Mike Vrabel

19. The Steelers traded offensive tackle Todd Fordham to the Carolina Panthers for a seventh-round pick and then selected a defensive lineman who spent four seasons with the Steelers and Buffalo Bills without ever playing in a single game. Who did Pittsburgh take with the 228th draft pick?

    a. Shaun Nua

    b. Bo Lacy

    c. Fred Gibson

    d. Drew Caylor

20. In the summer of 2017, the Steelers traded which wide receiver and a seventh-round pick to the Cleveland Browns for a sixth-round selection?

    a. Dri Archer

    b. Markus Wheaton

    c. Demarcus Ayers

    d. Sammie Coates

QUIZ ANSWERS

1. C - Santonio Holmes

2. A - True

3. B - Brad Wing

4. D - Vance McDonald

5. C - Mason Rudolph

6. A - Diontae Johnson & Zach Gentry

7. B - False

8. D - Minkah Fitzpatrick

9. C - May 14, 1968

10. B - Casey Hampton & Kendrell Bell

11. D - Byron Leftwich

12. A - True

13. C - Bryant McFadden

14. B - Troy Polamalu

15. D - Ricardo Colclough

16. A - True

17. C - Jerome Bettis

18. B - Jeremy Staat

19. A - Shaun Nua

20. D - Sammie Coates

DID YOU KNOW?

1. When punter Brad Wing was traded to the New York Giants after losing his job in a punting competition, the Steelers used the seventh-round pick to draft University of Houston receiver Demarcus Ayers. He finished his lone season with the franchise with 6 catches for 53 yards and 1 touchdown.

2. The Steelers and Kansas City Chiefs collaborated on one of the best trades in the history of the Pittsburgh franchise. During the 2003 NFL Draft, Kansas City received the 27th, 92nd and 200th pick for their 16th pick. The Steelers selected future Hall of Fame safety Troy Polamalu, while the Chiefs selected running back Larry Johnson at No 27 and defensive back Julian Battle at No. 92 before flipping the 200th pick to the Jets, who selected Brooks Bollinger. Only Johnson enjoyed success in the league for the Chiefs, earning a pair of Pro Bowl selections.

3. Pittsburgh traded a pair of draft picks – the 44th and 107th – to the Indianapolis Colts in 2004 for their 38th pick. The Steelers drafted defensive back Ricardo Colclough from tiny Tusculum University. He played just 43 games with the franchise and contributed 1 interception and 2.5 sacks. The Colts drafted strong safety Bob Sanders, who was named the 2007 NFL Defensive Player of the Year. Their other pick, linebacker Kendyll Pope, struggled with suspensions during his brief NFL career.

4. In 2006, the Steelers traded up seven spots to grab Ohio State wide receiver Santonio Holmes. The New York Giants received three draft picks from the Steelers and selected defensive end Mathias Kiwanuka (32nd), linebacker Gerris Wilkinson and offensive tackle Guy Whimper. Holmes was the MVP of Super Bowl XLIII, but was dealt to the New York Jets in 2010. Kiwanuka recorded 38.5 sacks in nine seasons, while Wilkinson won a Super Bowl ring but never contributed much on the field in a short career. Whimper played in 78 career games and signed with the Steelers as a free agent in 2013.

5. Pittsburgh traded their second-round and fourth-round picks in 2009 to the Denver Broncos for a pair of third-round selections. The Steelers drafted guard Kraig Urbik and speedy wide receiver Mike Wallace. Urbik was released by the Steelers in 2010, while Wallace played four seasons with the franchise before signing with Miami as a free agent. The Broncos drafted tight end Richard Quinn and guard Seth Olsen. Neither fared very well in the NFL.

6. The Steelers and Philadelphia Eagles swapped players in 2013. Pittsburgh dealt linebacker Adrian Robinson for running back Felix Jones and was considered the winner of the trade. Robinson bounced around with several teams and finished his career with just three tackles. Jones spent only one season with the Steelers and rushed for 184 yards in a backup role.

7. In a rare trade involving a kicker, the Steelers acquired Jacksonville Jaguars kicker Josh Scobee for a sixth-round

pick after both Shaun Suisham and Garrett Hartley suffered season-ending injuries. He missed a pair of field goals in Week 4 and was cut two days later. Jacksonville drafted quarterback Brandon Allen with the 201st pick, but he was released during training camp.

8. Pittsburgh fleeced the Arizona Cardinals in 2010 in a very lopsided trade. The Steelers shipped their fifth-round pick to the Cards for cornerback Bryant McFadden, who had previously played for the team from 2005-2008, and a sixth-round draft pick. Arizona selected Fordham quarterback John Skelton, who finished a lackluster career with only 15 touchdown passes. McFadden racked up 91 tackles in 29 games during his second stint with Pittsburgh, and the Steelers selected wide receiver Antonio Brown with the 195th pick. The dominating pass catcher electrified Pittsburgh fans before getting traded to the Raiders in 2019.

9. The Steelers traded center Sean Mahan to the Tampa Bay Buccaneers in 2008 for a 2009 seventh-round draft pick. Mahan had inked a five-year, $17 million deal with Pittsburgh and started all 16 games in 2007. However, Pittsburgh signed free agent Justin Hartwig the following offseason. The Steelers used the pick from the Buccaneers to draft center A.Q. Shipley. He was signed to the practice squad before being poached by the Philadelphia Eagles the following season. He has played in 105 NFL games so far during his career, including 70 starts.

10. During the 2018 NFL Draft, Pittsburgh traded talented but troubled wide receiver Martavis Bryant to the Oakland

Raiders. Due to injuries and off-field issues, Bryant only played in eight games for the Raiders before getting booted out of the league. The Steelers packaged the draft pick they received from the Raiders to move up three spots to select Oklahoma State quarterback Mason Rudolph.

CHAPTER 13:

SUPER BOWL SPECIAL

QUIZ TIME!

1. I broke Larry Csonka's record by rushing for 158 yards in Super Bowl IX and was named MVP. Who am I?

    a. Rocky Bleier
    b. John Fuqua
    c. Franco Harris
    d. Preston Pearson

2. The famed Steel Curtain defense shut out Fran Tarkenton and the Vikings offense to capture their first NFL title with a 16-6 victory in Super Bowl IX.

    a. True
    b. False

3. Green Bay Packer legend Bart Starr was the first quarterback to win back-to-back Super Bowl MVP awards. Who was the second quarterback to accomplish this feat?

    a. Bobby Layne
    b. Neil O'Donnell

c. Ben Roethlisberger

d. Terry Bradshaw

4. The Pittsburgh Steelers franchise suffered their first Super Bowl loss in Super Bowl XXX at the hands of which team?

   a. Green Bay Packers

   b. Dallas Cowboys

   c. Seattle Seahawks

   d. Los Angeles Rams

5. Which undrafted free agent raced 75 yards for a key touchdown to help the Steelers knock off the Seattle Seahawks in Super Bowl XL?

   a. Jon Whitman

   b. Tim Lester

   c. Willie Parker

   d. Rashard Mendenhall

6. President Bill Clinton appointed Super Bowl X MVP Lynn Swann as the Chairman of the President's Council on Physical Fitness and Sports.

   a. True

   b. False

7. Five Steelers have earned Most Valuable Player honors. Which of the following players has NOT been named a Super Bowl MVP?

   a. Antonio Brown

   b. Hines Ward

   c. Santonio Holmes

   d. Franco Harris

8. Which Steelers quarterback tossed two key interceptions in Super Bowl XXX as the franchise tasted defeat in an NFL title game for the first time?

    a. Charlie Batch
    b. Kordell Stewart
    c. Ben Roethlisberger
    d. Neil O'Donnell

9. Who is currently the youngest NFL coach to win a Super Bowl?

    a. Bill Cowher
    b. Chuck Noll
    c. Mike Tomlin
    d. Sean McVay

10. Pittsburgh was the first team to win six Super Bowls.

    a. True
    b. False

11. Steelers linebacker James Harrison set a Super Bowl record with a long interception return for a touchdown in Super Bowl XLIII. How many yards did Harrison ramble for the touchdown?

    a. 85
    b. 100
    c. 90
    d. 95

12. I was only 23 years old when I became the youngest quarterback to start and to win a Super Bowl. Who am I?

a. Tom Brady

b. Terry Bradshaw

c. Pat Mahomes

d. Ben Roethlisberger

13. Santonio Holmes hauled in the game-winning touchdown pass with less than a minute on the clock to help the Steelers edge the Arizona Cardinals, 27-23. How many seconds were left in the contest after Holmes' late-game heroics?

a. 27

b. 30

c. 35

d. 41

14. Chuck Noll was the second coach to lead his team to four Super Bowl victories.

a. True

b. False

15. Pittsburgh has had three wide receivers named Super Bowl MVP. Which of the following receivers has NOT won this prestigious award?

a. John Stallworth

b. Lynn Swann

c. Hines Ward

d. Santonio Holmes

16. The Steelers defeated the Dallas Cowboys in Super Bowl X behind their famed Steel Curtain defense. How many times did Pittsburgh sack Hall of Fame quarterback Roger Staubach?

a. 4

b. 6

c. 7

d. 3

17. Who caught Terry Bradshaw's last Super Bowl TD pass against the Los Angeles Rams in 1980?

a. Lynn Swann

b. Randy Grossman

c. John Stallworth

d. Benny Cunningham

18. Who intercepted a Roger Staubach pass in the end zone on the final play of the game to clinch the Steelers victory over the Dallas Cowboys in Super Bowl X?

a. Donnie Shell

b. Glen Edwards

c. Mel Blount

d. J.T. Thomas

19. L.C. Greenwood tallied a team-high 4 sacks in four Super Bowl games.

a. True

b. False

20. Which of the following Steelers running backs never scored a touchdown in a Super Bowl?

a. Bam Morris

b. Jerome Bettis

c. Willie Parker

QUIZ ANSWERS

1. C - Franco Harris

2. A - True

3. D - Terry Bradshaw

4. B - Dallas Cowboys

5. C - Willie Parker

6. B - False

7. A - Antonio Brown

8. D - Neil O'Donnell

9. C - Mike Tomlin

10. A - True

11. B - 100

12. D - Ben Roethlisberger

13. C - 35

14. B - False

15. A - John Stallworth

16. C - 7

17. C - John Stallworth

18. B - Glen Edwards

19. B - False

20. B Jerome Bettis

DID YOU KNOW?

1. When Pittsburgh and the Green Bay Packers squared off in Super Bowl XLV, the Steelers had 25 players on their roster with Super Bowl rings. However, the lone player with Green Bay to have a ring was fullback John Kuhn. He was a member of the Steelers practice squad in 2005 and received a ring when Pittsburgh defeated the Seattle Seahawks in Super Bowl XL.

2. The Pittsburgh Steelers and the New England Patriots are tied for the most Super Bowl victories in NFL history with six apiece. The Steelers were the team of the 1970s with four Vince Lombardi Trophies, and they won Super Bowl XL and Super Bowl XLIII. The Patriots have won all their title since 2001, including three Super Bowl wins in a span of five seasons, from 2015 to 2019.

3. Despite guiding the Steelers to a 21-10 win over the Seattle Seahawks, Ben Roethlisberger had a horrible day passing. The 23-year-old became the youngest quarterback to start and win a Super Bowl game but completed only 9 of 21 passes for 123 yards and 2 interceptions. His 22.6 passer rating set a Super Bowl record for the lowest passing rating to win a game.

4. The Steelers started the tradition of Super Bowl champions visiting the White House. In 1979, both the Steelers and the Pittsburgh Pirates held a joint ceremony with President

Jimmy Carter. The Steelers defeated the Los Angeles Rams in Super Bowl XIV and the Pittsburgh Pirates knocked off the Baltimore Orioles in the 1979 World Series.

5. Franco Harris is the all-time Super Bowl rushing leader with 354 yards and holds the Super Bowl record with 101 carries. He rushed for 158 yards and a touchdown in a 16-6 victory over the Minnesota Vikings in Super Bowl IX to earn Most Valuable Player honors.

6. The first points that the Pittsburgh franchise scored in a Super Bowl were delivered by Dwight White. The defensive end lost 20 pounds during the week leading up to Super Bowl IX due to pneumonia and was not expected to play. However, White not only played but gave the Steelers a 2-0 lead by blocking a punt that went through the back of the end zone for a safety.

7. The first rematch in Super Bowl history took place in Super Bowl XIII between the Steelers and Dallas Cowboys. The two teams, both with a pair of Super Bowl wins, also squared off in the Orange Bowl for a second time. The winner was set to be crowned the Team of the '70s, which Pittsburgh attained by dealing the Cowboys another Super Bowl loss.

8. Pittsburgh and the Los Angeles Rams set a record in Super Bowl XIV when 103,985 spectators trekked to the Rose Bowl to watch the big game. The Steelers rolled to a 31-19 victory as the Steel Curtain overcame three Terry Bradshaw interceptions to notch the franchise's record-setting fourth Vince Lombardi trophy.

9. A record three Pittsburgh receivers have been named Super Bowl MVP. Lynn Swann earned MVP honors with 4 catches for 161 yards and a touchdown in Super Bowl X. Hines Ward took home the MVP Award in Super Bowl XL with 5 catches for 123 yards and a touchdown. Santonio Holmes had 9 receptions for 131 yards, including the game-winning score with 35 seconds left in the game, to win the MVP award for Super Bowl XLIII.

10. Despite the Steelers having a legacy of Hall of Fame wide receivers, Andre Hastings holds the team record for most receptions in the Super Bowl. Hastings had a career day on the biggest stage in Super Bowl XXX against the Dallas Cowboys when he hauled in 10 passes for 98 yards. However, the Cowboys topped the Steelers in the Super Bowl for the first time, 27-17.

CONCLUSION

The Pittsburgh Steelers are one of the most successful teams in the history of the National Football League. A downtrodden franchise until the AFL-NFL merger, the Steelers won back-to-back Super Bowls on two occasions and were crowned the team of the 1970s. Pittsburgh added two more Vince Lombardi Trophies in 2006 and 2009, and is tied with the New England Patriots with six Super Bowl wins.

The architect of the Steelers dynasty in the 1970s was head coach Chuck Noll. A remarkable talent evaluator, Noll seemingly chose Hall-of-Famers in every draft. In a remarkable span from 1969-1974, he drafted Hall of Fame players in every draft except one. In what is arguably the best draft in NFL history, Noll drafted four future Hall-of-Famers with the Steelers' first five picks in the 1974 NFL Draft. He also signed an undrafted free agent that same year who went on to have a Hall of Fame career.

The number of legendary players to wear the black and gold is more than impressive. The famed "Steel Curtain" defense was led by Hall-of-Famers Mean Joe Greene, Jack Lambert, Jack Ham, Mel Blount and Donnie Shell. Other defensive players inducted into the Pro Football Hall of Fame include

Kevin Greene, Ernie Stautner, Troy Polamalu and Rod Woodson to name just a few.

The fortunes of the Steeler offense changed dramatically with the arrivals of Hall-of-Famers Terry Bradshaw, Franco Harris, Lynn Swann, John Stallworth and Dermontti Dawson. Other offensive stars who were inducted into Canton are Jerome Bettis, Mike Webster, John Henry Johnson, Bobby Layne and many more.

This book is a tribute to the players, coaches and fans who bleed black and gold. The Pittsburgh Steelers have their sights set on winning more Super Bowls, and the people of the Steel City could not be more excited.

Made in the USA
Monee, IL
14 October 2022

15827398R00075